D0318687

A NORTHERN
COAST TO COAST WALK

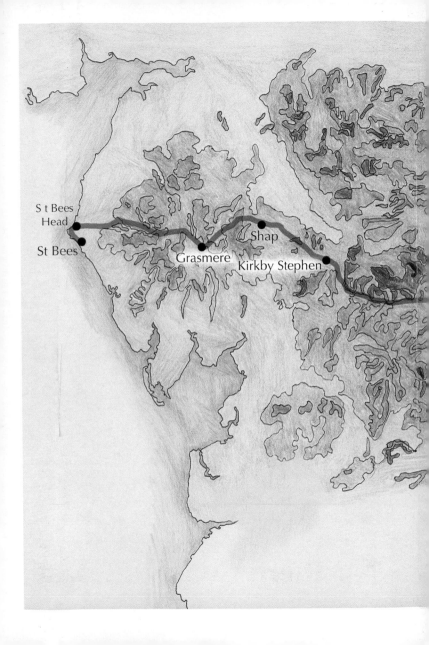

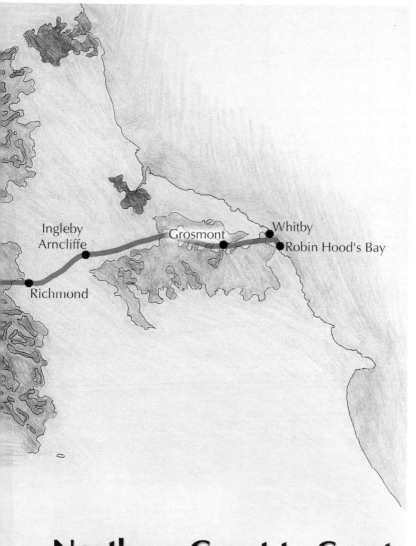

Northern Coast to Coast

About the Author

A writer and photographer since 1983, Terry Marsh specialises in the outdoors, the countryside, walking and travel worldwide. He is the author of 40+ books including the award-winning Cicerone guides to the *Shropshire Way* (1999), and guides to the *Pennine Way*, the *Dales Way*, the *Severn Way* and *The West Highland Way* (1997 and 2003).

Terry is a Fellow of the Royal Geographical Society (FRGS), and the Society of Antiquaries of Scotland (FSA Scot), and a Member of the Society of Authors, MENSA, NUJ and the British Guild of Travel Writers. He is a regular contributor to various magazines, including *Quicksilver* (Walks Editor), *Dalesman*, *Cumbria*, *Peak District*, and occasional contributor (words and pictures) to *In Britain* and *Living France*. Terry lectures on 'Writing about Travel' at Burton Manor College, Wirral and Alston Hall College, Longridge. He is also the annual revision author for internet city guides to Copenhagen, Strasbourg, Cannes, Avignon and Lyon for www.worldtravelguide.net.

Widely travelled, Terry's main areas of interest are England (especially The Chilterns AONB; Cumbria, Lake District, Peak District, Lancashire, Oxfordshire and the Yorkshire Dales); Scotland (especially the islands, including St Kilda); Isle of Man; Wales; France; Australia; the countryside generally; walking; food and wine.

A NORTHERN COAST TO COAST WALK
HANDBOOK AND ACCOMMODATION GUIDE

by

Terry Marsh

CICERONE

2 POLICE SQUARF, MILNTHORPE, CUMBRIA, LA7 7PY
www.cicerone.co.uk

© Terry Marsh 1993, 2003
Reprinted 1997
Second edition 2003
Reprinted 2004

British Cataloguing-in-Publication Data.
A catalogue record for this book is available from the British Library.
ISBN 1 85284 367 5

DEDICATED TO THE
MEMORY OF JUMBO

Advice to Readers

Readers are advised that while every effort is taken by the author to ensure the accuracy of this guidebook, changes can occur which may affect the contents. It is advisable to check locally on transport, accommodation, shops, etc, but even right of way can be altered.

The publisher would welcome notes of any such changes.

Front cover: Approaching Boredale Hause in the Lake District

CONTENTS

ACKNOWLEDGEMENTS

By the end of the walk, the 'support team' had grown to Himalayan proportions, or so it seemed. My then wife, Gaynor, accompanied me all of the way, and discovered at least twenty-five different localities suitable for retirement! And though residential fantasies became a note of levity throughout the work, her companionship and support, both out there and at home, were of more serious stuff, and valuable beyond measure.

My friend Dennis Kelsall was of immense assistance, checking all my measurements of distances and ascents, reading the manuscript, personally plumbing the depth of at least four bogs, and generally stuffing his face with everything edible that couldn't run away, from mushrooms to plums, from sloes to wild strawberries. His wife, Jan, and her parents, Jim and Sheila, accompanied us for many of the days, as did Ron, and Jumbo the Dog. To all of them I owe a considerable debt of gratitude. Sadly, Jumbo died in 1993, and is still greatly missed though Ron has recently replaced him with a youthful bundle of canine mischief. Jim died recently, too.

When it came to facts, information, route revisions, logistical support I was amazed by, and immensely grateful for, the willing help I received from many people I now feel obliged to acknowledge: Andrew Nicholson and Dick Capel of the East Cumbria Countryside Project helped painstakingly with route changes and waymarking between Shap and Whitsundale; Sue Arnott, formerly Access Officer with the Yorkshire Dales National Park, and Joanne Coote with the North York Moors National Park both gave considerable help and time, as did Sue Tunnicliff, Youth Hostels Association, and Kim Robbins, English Heritage. Local help came from many sources: David Kerr of the Forestry Commission, Ennerdale Bridge; Christine Strickland, Kendal Library; Dr Paul Bond, Reeth; Bob Watson, then of The White Swan, Danby Wiske; John Negus, Kirkby Fleetham and Peter Penny, North Yorkshire County Council.

Without the support and help of everyone, the guide would have been a less accurate, less valuable work. When I came to revise the accommodation guide it was good to hear so many friendly and familiar voices again.

INTRODUCTION

Sock-patterned feet slowly turning a brighter shade of pale in the chilly waters of the Swale, we perched precariously on rocks not far from Isles Bridge, lunch boxes plundered and Trangias working overtime to quench the demand for fresh-brewed tea. Among the polished rocks a bright green beetle scurried by on its daily business, destined to remain on the tiny river islet until the next flood carried it away, while among the branches of a nearby bush a spider industriously repaired a web damaged by last night's winds. A nesting wren scolded us from the undergrowth, where red admirals, tortoiseshells and gatekeepers flitted about on their endless toil, as from the riverbank came the calls of oystercatchers, dippers, grey wagtails and sand martins. Everywhere nature was at work: only we four were at play, our hearts and minds now, well into the walk, fully attuned to the fine detail around us.

At first our preoccupation had been with rasping lungs, aching legs and shoulders, and the next excruciating step. But that, we knew, was only the beginning, as it is on any long, heavily-laden walk, and within days those pain-oriented sensations, about which we made more than was justified, were not even a memory. Instead, the senses began to hear the rivers and becks, to detect the heady perfume of honeysuckle and broom, the gentle touch of gossamer, and to spot the slightest movement among the hedgerows and along the fellsides. Long before we had half crossed the Lake District, the transformation was complete, we were walkers once more, and looking forward with confidence to crossing England on foot.

Grisedale Tarn

A NORTHERN COAST TO COAST WALK

In 1973 Alfred Wainwright, guide-book writer extraordinaire, turned his attention to devising a walk across northern England, from coast to coast. Though far from an original concept – walkers had been travelling coast to coast across Scotland, for example, for years – it nevertheless sparked many an imagination, and raised a few lethargic bottoms from comfy armchairs, in the process. His chosen route was but one of many possibilities, and the man himself encouraged walkers to devise their own. So, the present walk differs significantly in a number of ways. Being environmentally and ecologically more friendly, it ostracises much of the road-walking that bedevilled Wainwright's plan, and overcomes the indifference he often displayed towards rights-of-way, or the lack of them. What results is a tantalising and inspiring excursion to rank with the finest of this country's

long distance walks, and all of it on established rights of way or permissive paths.

The walk runs from the Irish Sea lapping the shores of Cumbria at St Bees, to where the waters of the North Sea flow into Robin Hood's Bay on the Yorkshire Coast, a distance of just under 285 kilometres (178 miles). Not a walk on which to cut one's teeth as a backpacker (the Dales Way would be much more fitting for that), but one on which seasoned walkers will experience little difficulty.

Opening with a lofty scamper around the edge of St Bees Head, the first day, usually taken as far as Ennerdale Bridge, samples the delights of coastal walking before heading inland to the western fringe of Lakeland. The leg-buckling slopes of the minor summit, Dent Fell, on a warm day especially, come as something of a joke, but beyond that one of Lakeland's hidden gems, Uldale and Nannycatch Beck, compensates amply on the run in to Ennerdale.

Crossing South Head, St Bees

Haweswater Fells, near Burnbanks

Ennerdale marks the entry, if you like, to Lakeland proper, and pushes far into the heart of steep-sided mountains, to the great summits of Pillar and Great Gable that lie at its head. Then with a daunting flourish, the walk engages the short-lived wrath of Loft Beck as it hauls itself across the fells to Borrowdale, coming first by a back road into Seatoller, and then by a charming traverse to Rosthwaite, as much on the traditional tourist route as Black Sail Youth Hostel in the deep sanctum of Ennerdale is off it.

By enterprising leaps, the walk visits Langstrath, crosses by Greenup Edge to Far Easedale and Grasmere, before continuing to Patterdale via Grisedale Tarn. Variant possibilities arise: a diversion over Dollywaggon Pike to Helvellyn, if you wish, or an airy traverse of St Sunday Crag.

Beyond Patterdale the route clings as long as it can to the high ground before throwing in its hand and dropping to the shores of Haweswater, preparing, inevitably, to leave the beauties of Lakeland behind.

There may be a temptation to think that once the Lake District has been left behind, the finest walking has gone. If the truth is known, what lies ahead is every bit as enchanting, captivating, and spiritually reviving as Lakeland; qualities derived, if not from the ruggedness of the landscape, then from its sublime insinuation into our senses, its soft, and outstandingly beautiful insistence on playing its part in this drama, with equal rights to top billing. And quite rightly so!

The sensitivity of the landscape and the environment between Shap and Kirkby Stephen has led to the route being waymarked in order to protect important areas. Beyond Kirkby Stephen the problem is one of erosion. To help minimise this, the ascent of Nine Standards Rigg goes by way of Faraday Gill, and then by Whitsundale to Keld at the head of Swaledale, arguably one of the finest of the dales.

Preferring a lofty traverse between

River Swale

Keld and Reeth, the walk makes what it can of the old mining routes that abound in this historically fascinating region, while, for those who prefer a valley line, the flower-decked meadows along the River Swale are second to none. Between Reeth and Richmond limestone scars, leafy lanes, woodland and rich pastures are the order of the day, while Richmond itself seems to remain aloof of the twenty-first century in many ways, retaining much of its great historical flavour, centred on its castle.

The ensuing Vale of Mowbray forms a lengthy link between the Dales and the North York Moors, and though approaching marathon distance does have room for inventive shortcuts. As the day goes on, so the Cleveland Hills approach, and an unrivalled crossing of the North York Moors lies in wait. Superb views enliven the way, which here proves rather more undulating than might be expected.

Beyond Clay Bank Top the walking is effortless, with only the pull on to Urra Moor demanding any effort. After that, leg-swinging freedom, partly along the line of a former mineral railway, is the order of the day with expansive views across rolling moorland to cheer the spirit, and prepare for the final stage of the journey.

The concluding stage is as fitting as the first, and finds its way along old toll roads, by way of ancient burial mounds, across tracts of heather moorland, through ancient, time-worn villages, delightful woodland, until, at the very end, we are faced, as we were in the beginning, with an exhilarating clifftop walk to the beauty that is Robin Hood's Bay.

The Coast to Coast Walk is, as Keats observed:

'A thing of beauty...a joy forever'

Make sure you experience it. Amen.

EXPLANATORY NOTES

Distances and Ascent: To ensure accuracy when giving distances and ascent, detailed measurements have been made using OS Pathfinder and Outdoor Leisure Maps, at a scale of 1:25,000, where necessary measuring distances at 100-metre intervals, and calculating vertical heights to within five metres. Any lack of precision that this gives is unlikely to cause distress to walkers accustomed to regular outings over mountain and moorland terrain.

Using the Guide: Following this Introduction the Guide is found in three sections. The first gives the route description, from west to east, annotated as appropriate with notes of geological, historical, industrial, sociological and natural history interest. The second section gives the route description only in an east to west direction, cross-referenced to the west–east description for explanations of points interest or comment. The final section comprises of an Accommodation Guide, list of

Crossing the moor above Swinner Gill (high level route)

Doctors, Dentists and list of Useful Addresses.

The main route description is given in plain lettering in the text, while general comments are in italic type. The author's comments, observations, and general background information are given in green type. These occur in the main text in the order in which they are encountered along the walk.

Where variant routes are given, these are indented and have a green sideline running along the outside edge of the page.

Although the guide is written in five sections, no real attempt has been made to construct 'day length' sections, that is for the individual walker. As a rule however, each stretch ends at a location where accommodation, of one sort or another, may be found; occasionally, where this practice has not been followed religiously, a note appears in the text wherever accommodation is

close at hand. (See also 'Planning the Walk' below.)

PLANNING THE WALK

Walkers with other long distance walks under their belts will find that the Coast to Coast differs very little in terms of physical effort and organisation, but, as always, good forward planning and attention to detail can prevent a happy and rewarding endeavour from turning into a nightmare.

The first prerequisite is to plan days you can realistically complete laden with a pack, and even then to be prepared to modify your intentions should optimism have gained the better of sound judgement. There is simply no joy in plodding on at a fixed distance day after day, unless you are addicted to route marches, while to work out a crossing which allows no time to take in the splendid scenery, to explore and potter about, to dangle feet in streams and rivers, to visit the many pubs, churches, and sites of historical interest is to relegate the quintessential elements of the walk to mere coincidence, and to elevate the laudable but otherwise simple and unoriginal concept of walking from one coast of Britain to the other to a peerage is does not deserve.

As a general guide you will need about two weeks for the walk, give or take a day or so, plus whatever time is need to get to and from start and finish points. The total distance is 285 kilometres (178 miles), and involves an ascent (and descent) of 6,995 metres (22,825 feet), no mean undertaking. This gives an average daily walk of 20 kilometres (12 miles), with 496 metres (1,630 feet) of ascent, quite a comfortable proposition for walkers accustomed to long distance and undertakings, while others may find some sense in first 'cutting their teeth' on a walk of lesser dimensions,

like the Dales Way, for example – though even that should not be underestimated.

To avoid imposing any set pattern on the walk beyond that demanded by the disposition of accommodation, no attempt has been made to configure the guide into daily sections, though the whole book has been constructed in five sections, of nominal geographical significance. As a rule, each section simply represents a linking together of two or more places that provide accommodation in some shape or form. Given this format the walker can, and should, construct his or her own daily dosage, according to individual standards of fitness and competence, and the inclination to wander and explore.

All this pre-supposes walkers want to do the whole thing from end to end in the one endeavour, and this is a commendable and logical challenge, but the Coast to Coast does, with a little ingenuity, lend itself to

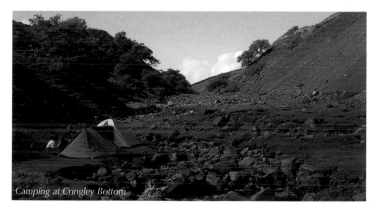

Camping at Cringley Bottom

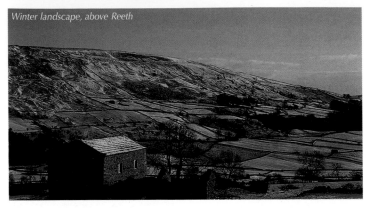
Winter landscape, above Reeth

completion on a piecemeal basis, and I have had many reports from walkers who have done just that, and enjoyably so: indeed, it was the basis on which this guide was researched. There are generally good public transport services along much of the walk, though equally there are some isolated spots that need careful planning to reach. Only a modicum of cooperation is all that is needed, however, for groups of walkers with at least two cars to devise linear excursions.

Public transport is available at both ends of the walk. St Bees is on the rail network, linking with Carlisle (north) and Barrow, for Lancaster (south). And though Robin Hood's Bay lost its railway some time ago, it is served by a bus service connecting Whitby and Scarborough, both of which have railway stations. Of the two, Scarborough has the slightly better connections, with a good service running through to York.

One tip, perhaps of key importance, with regard to planning day lengths, is to decide in advance the time and day at which you hope to finish, and adjust the final few days to make that possible. It could also determine the time and day at which you start. This is true whichever way you make the crossing. Glaisdale to Robin Hood's Bay is some 29 kilometres (18 miles) with 500 metres (1,640 feet) of ascent; is that how you want to finish the walk? Or would it be more sensible to start the last day at Grosmont or Hawsker, for example? Or to head straight for Robin Hood's Bay by road once Hawsker is left? By making these slight adjustments you may well find that you force a shorter than average day somewhere in the middle, and that might be no bad thing!

On such a crossing inevitably you meet people from many different backgrounds and cultures, but very few who will not take an interest in your welfare and your adventure. Accompanying this book is an Accommodation Guide, and many of the proprietors listed in it have demonstrated a willingness to help walkers to enjoy their individual adventure; running walkers to pubs and restaurants, helping with laundry and drying arrangements, picking people up from remote spots, ferrying packs about, and so on. These are all part of a special culture that is beginning to embrace the walk, and a nice thing it is, too!

MAPS

The following maps will be needed:

EITHER 1:50,000 Landranger Series

Sheet 89	West Cumbria
Sheet 90	Penrith, Keswick and Ambleside area
Sheet 91	Appleby-in-Westmorland area
Sheet 92	Barnard Castle and surrounding area
Sheet 93	Middlesbrough and Darlington area
Sheet 94	Whitby and surrounding area
Sheet 98	Wensleydale and Upper Wharfedale
Sheet 99	Northallerton, Ripon and surrounding area

OR the following EXPLORER maps at 1:25,000

303	Whitehaven & Workington, Cockermouth
OL 4	English Lakes, North Western area
OL 7	English Lakes, South Eastern area (to a limited extent only)
OL 5	English Lakes, North Eastern area
OL 19	Howgill Fells and Upper Eden Valley
OL 30	Yorkshire Dales – Northern and Central areas
304	Darlington & Richmond, Egglescliffe
302	Northallerton & Thirsk, Catterick & Bedale
OL 26	North York moors – Western area
OL 27	North York Moors – Eastern area

Harveys also produce a series of maps that cover the Lake District, and while these are of excellent quality, produced on waterproof material, they have limited suitability, for anyone undertaking the Coast to Coast Walk. If you have them, however, you may find that you can do without one or more of the OS Outdoor Leisure Maps.

FACILITIES ALONG THE WAY

The Coast to Coast Packhorse

Public transport is limited in rural areas. To help with this, and to ease the crossing for walkers, private enterprise has developed a Coast to Coast Packhorse service, which will shuttle your pack to your evening's destination. Pick up points, subject to

Across the southern slopes of Great Ewe Fell

alteration, are at St Bees, Ennerdale, Borrowdale, Grasmere, Patterdale, Shap, Orton, Kirkby Stephen, Keld, Reeth, Richmond, Danby Wiske, Ingleby Cross, Great Broughton, Blakey, Glaisdale, Grosmont and Robin Hood's Bay.

In addition, the company operates a mini bus service to transport walkers to the start of the walk at St Bees and return from Robin Hood's Bay, having parked their vehicles at the company base at Kirby Stephen.

For details of these services contact the Coast to Coast Packhorse, Littlethwaite, North Stainmore, Kirkby Stephen, Cumbria CA17 4EX (017683 42028); Email: packhorse@cumbria.com; Website: www.cumbria.com/packhorse

Railway service

St Bees, Kirkby Stephen, Glaisdale, Egton Bridge, Grosmont, Sleights.

Post Offices

St Bees, Sandwith, Moor Row, Cleator, Ennerdale Bridge, Rosthwaite, Stonethwaite, Grasmere, Glenridding, Patterdale, Bampton, Shap, Orton, Kirkby Stephen, Muker, Gunnerside, Reeth, Grinton, Richmond, Colburn, Brompton-on-Swale, East Harsley, Ingleby Cross, Osmotherly, Swainby, Carlton, Great Broughton, Glaisdale, Grosmont, Sleights, Hawsker, Robin Hood's Bay.

Public Conveniences

St Bees, Seatoller, Rosthwaite, Grasmere, Glenridding, Patterdale, Shap, Kirkby Stephen, Keld, Muker, Gunnerside, Low Row, Reeth, Grinton, Richmond, Osmotherly, Swainby, Carlton Bank, Glaisdale, Egton Bridge, Grosmont, Sleights, Robin Hood's Bay.

Telephones

St Bees, Moor Row, Cleator, Ennerdale Bridge, Gillerthwaite, Seatoller, Rosthwaite, Stonethwaite, Grasmere, Glenridding, Patterdale, Burnbanks, Bampton, Rosgill, Shap, Orton, Raisbeck, Newbiggin-on-Lune, Kirkby Stephen, Hartley, Keld, Muker, Ivelet, Gunnerside, Low Row, Healaugh, Reeth, Grinton, Marrick, Marske, Richmond, Colburn, Brompton-on-Swale, Catterick Bridge, Bolton-on-Swale, Streetlam, Danby Wiske, Oaktree Hill, East Harsley, Ingleby Cross, Osmotherly, Swainby, Huthwaite Green, Carlton Bank, Carlton, Great Broughton, Glaisdale, Egton Bridge, Grosmont, Sleights, Littlebeck, Hawsker, Robin Hood's Bay.

ACCOMMODATION

Bed and Breakfast, Youth Hostels, Campsites, Barns, Inns – see the Accommodation Guide in the appendices for details.

The Northern Coast to Coast Walk is amply furnished with inexpensive bed and breakfast accommodation throughout its length, only becoming sparse between Patterdale and Keld, and there is a good string of camping facilities also. So that walkers may always have an up-to-date listing of bed and breakfast and other accommodation opportunities an Accommodation Guide accompanies this Handbook. Walkers who find other accommodation (of any type) worthy of inclusion

Approaching Nine Standards Rigg via Faraday Gill

in the guide, please write to the author c/o the publisher. Sadly, the effects of foot and mouth disease during 2001 have meant that quite a few B&Bs have gone out of business.

The author would also welcome information on properties found unworthy of inclusion, giving details, so that these may be removed from the list.

EQUIPMENT

All walkers have their own preferences in the matter of equipment and clothing. When extending day-walking into multiple day-walking much the same general items are needed, but some thought needs to be given to matters of personal comfort in the hygiene department.

The following list may be found a useful reminder – rucsack (comfortable, well-padded, and appropriate to backpacking rather than day-walking), boots, socks (and spare socks), trousers (or shorts, etc.), underclothes, shirt, midwear (eg. pullover) and spare, wind-waterproof jacket and over-trousers, hat, gloves, maps, compass, torch (with spare battery and bulbs), whistle, first-aid kit, survival bag or space blanket, food and drink, insect repellent, ablution tackle, including half a roll of toilet tissue (for emergencies), small hand towel.

Campers will also need such additional weighty items as tent, sleeping bag, Karrimat, cooking equipment and utensils.

Pedal bin liners will be found to have a number of useful purposes: keeping wet clothing separate from dry in the rucsack, containing burst packets of food, cereal, etc., and rubbish, until a suitable disposal point can be reached, and for insulating dry socks from wet boots when walking.

And if you can manage the extra weight, why not take a small notebook, and infuriate everyone else by keeping a daily log you steadfastly refuse to let them read! Think about taking a suitable book to read in the evenings, but not on the scale of *War and Peace*.

MONEY

One final point worth considering: for much of the walk there is extremely limited opportunity to avail yourself of 'hole-in-the-wall' cash dispensers, and not everyone accepts credit cards. A cheque book and banker's card, however, can usually be used to obtain cash at post offices.

1. ACROSS LAKELAND

ST BEES

On close inspection of St Bees we find the village to be larger than expected, and endowed with a history of considerable interest. Its church is the oldest and finest in what was West Cumberland; its school quite ancient, as is its bridge. But of most interest is the story of St Bega, one of much charm and with all the hallmarks of a fairy tale.

The earliest records about **St Bega** are to be found in the *Life and Miracles of St Bega the Virgin* now preserved in the British Museum, and dating from the twelfth century. Material from this work comes, the author claims, from the narrative of reliable men, a significant comment in the light of the latter-day claims that she never really existed.

Bega was the daughter of an Irish king, and determined to remain a lifelong virgin, a decision reinforced by a dream in which she received from a stranger an arm-ring bearing the sign of the holy cross. Bega's father, however, was equally determined she should marry a Norwegian prince, a proposition so abhorrent to Bega that she fled across the sea with a company of nuns seeking peace and solitude, and landed in a wooded region, near present-day St Bees. Here there probably existed a primitive Christian community, for the name

As if to protect its splendid setting from prying eyes, St Bees lies huddled shyly away in a valley near the sea, a grey village of antiquity and charm. The valley is that of Pow Beck, a direct link with the busy industrialisation of Whitehaven to the north. Approaching from the south, however, it is always with an element of surprise that the village springs into view, from a distance possessing the quiet, unassuming air of a Scottish crofting community in the way the buildings, resting on the backdrop of St Bees Head, seem to lie at one, in harmony with the landscape.

At the start: St Bees

21

The church of St Mary and St Bega is an exquisite place. Its greatest glory, the west doorway, a deeply recessed, richly columned and decorative portal, dates from about 1160, and is a splendid example of late Norman work. The church contains a number of late Norman coffin slabs, while in the transept is a beautifully incised effigy of Lady Johanna Lucy, who died in 1369; in the churchyard rest two mutilated thirteenth-century knights, one bearing a shield with the arms of Ireby on it. Of more recent times, there is a touching monument of a child of four on a tomb under a recess, a disquieting little figure as she lies asleep, a spray of lilies in her hand.

Preston, 'priest town', was given by Anglians to land between what is now St Bees and Whitehaven; later this land was granted to the Priory of St Mary and the Virgin Bega at its foundation in 1120. The industrious effort of Bega and her nuns brought its rewards as slowly they established a nunnery on the site of the present Priory Church. The nunnery survived two centuries before being plundered by Danish raiders. Much later, after its foundation, the Priory Church of St Mary suffered a similar fate at the hands of Scottish raiders, in due course ending its days in much the same manner as numerous other monastic buildings, under the dissolution decree of Henry VIII.

Although it is claimed by some that Bega was a mythical character arising from the pagan Nordic custom, in vogue with the nineteenth century, of swearing oaths on a sacred arm-ring, the 'bracelet of the blessed Virgin Bega, kept in the priory church,' on which oaths were taken, is mentioned in no less than six charters recorded in the early thirteenth century.

The *Life and Miracles* does not mention that Bega was shipwrecked on the Cumberland coast, or that a nunnery was founded, these details apparently being added in the seventeenth century by one Edmund Sandford. Sandford also wrote: 'There was a pious religious Lady Abbess and some of her sisters driven in by storm at Whitehaven and ship cast away i'the harbour.' The Abbess begged assistance from the Lady of Egremont whose Lord promised the nuns as much land as snow fell upon the next morning 'bein midsumerday'. In pre-global warming days, snow did indeed often remain as late as mid-summer, and, not surprisingly therefore, though he must have been a little taken aback, the next day the morning saw the land for three miles to the sea covered with snow. 'And thereupon builded this St Bees Abbie and gave the land was snowen unto it and the town and haven of Whitehaven' with other dues and further lands. Obviously, a man of his word.

St Bees School, entered through a beautiful memorial gate, was founded in 1583 by Archbishop Edmund Grindal of Canterbury, a native of the district, by virtue of a charter of Queen Elizabeth. At first intended as a

Free Grammar School for local boys only, a restriction it maintained until 1879, it later widened its educational opportunities and opened its doors to others.

Buttressed by so much of interest and antiquity on the one hand and the swelling Irish Sea on the other, St Bees is both a fitting and inspiring overture to the walk, and a place to come back to when time is at less of a premium and the sense of urgency and enthusiasm for the impending departure no longer appropriate.

St Bees to Cleator

Distance: 13.6 kilometres (8.5 miles)
Ascent: 280 metres (920 feet)

Half a mile or so from the village centre, the beach of St Bees is the starting point for the Northern Coast to Coast Walk. Here the tourist has invaded the scene: car parks, toilets and a caravan site straggle the coastal frontage, and for the walker suddenly escape becomes a high priority.

The first section of the walk is across sandstone clifftops, rare in Cumbria, a fine elevated introduction on which to attune legs, lungs and mind. Beyond the coast, the mess of Whitehaven's industry is passed, thankfully in a brief passage, before the more relaxed agriculture landscape around Cleator that heralds the high fells and deep valleys of Lakeland.

But first, a touch of silliness or two: one a ceremonial dipping of the boots in the waves (let's hope the tide is in), an act to be repeated at Robin Hood's Bay; the other the selection of a small pebble, washed and fashioned by the waters of the Irish Sea, to be carried as a makeshift talisman throughout the journey and deposited where the waters of the North Sea can complete the process of erosion.

The sea wall, built to protect St Bees from the worst ravages of the sea, ends abruptly in a downfall of boulders and debris from the ever-crumbling cliffs, soon to be encountered. This is where the walk starts.

Here, cross Rottington Beck and the journey has

The whole of St Bees Head is formed from shales and sandstone, and dates from comparatively recent times in the geological evolution of the Lake District, between 135 and 225 million years ago. It is by far the most impressive feature on the Cumbrian coast, unless one's point of view can accord even greater impressiveness to the nuclear power plant at Sellafield!

begun, leaving the beach behind and climbing by a flight of wooden steps alongside the RSPB St Bees Head Nature Reserve. Height is gained rapidly, and with it, on a clear day, a widening panorama of far horizons.

To the south, beyond the towers of Sellafield, rise the whaleback summits of Black Combe and its acolytes; to the east the first tantalising glimpse of high Lakeland fells; while far out to sea, 50 kilometres (30+ miles) distant, the blue–purple form of the Isle of Man looms hazily from a shimmering sea.

Still ascending by a prominent path, the walk soon reaches the remains of a coastguard lookout post, where the suddenness of the drop to the shore impresses itself noticeably. St Bees Head is formed into two distinct halves, South Head and North Head, separated by

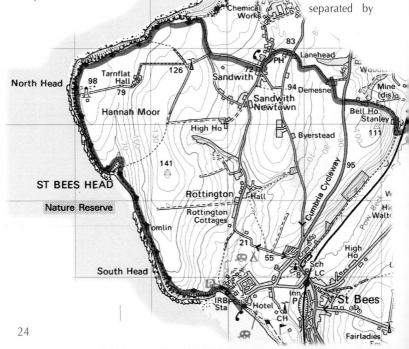

the fissure of Fleswick Bay, and as the gradient eases, near the top of South Head, the lighthouse on North Head springs into view.

At a stile the path moves away from the clifftop for a short while to follow the bottom edge of steeply sloping pastures, an easy stroll on flowery turf.

The openness of the view, the wheeling, swooping company of countless sea birds, and the flitting purpose of butterflies here arouse sensations of well-being and contentment, a perfect mental conditioning for what is to follow on the journey eastwards. Along the way a number of protected arenas have been constructed to facilitate observation of the sea birds that include gannet, kittiwake, guillemot, razorbill, puffin and black-backed gulls.

For the moment, however, the route lies northwards, easing downwards to Fleswick Bay.

Fleswick Bay cuts sharply into St Bees Head, forcing a return almost to sea level. A brief halt

would not be unwelcome or unjustified here, even so early in the walk, for the bay is a most beautiful part of the headland, famed for attractive pebbles, its hanging terraces of wild flowers, caves, colourful weathered rocks, and intimate views of towering sea cliffs.

A direct return may be made to the path above Fleswick

25

To the visiting eye the chemical works do indeed disfigure the landscape, but everything has to be seen in context. The great mound of land south of Whitehaven, technically known as Preston Isle, has had enormous influence on the prosperity of the town and its people. Beneath the surface have been found not only extensive coal measures, now largely worked-out, but large quantities of anhydrite, or calcium sulphate, which, suitably processed, can be used to manufacture sulphuric acid and cement. This 'buried treasure' has meant up to 2000 jobs in the area, and the importance of this, in a district that has known more than its fair share of unemployment, cannot be underestimated.

Bay, without having to retreat inland to the main stile, by locating a series of holds in the rocks ascending to a hurdle/stile; heavily-laden walkers still trying to find their backpacking legs might wisely opt, however, for rejoining the walk at the inland crossing point.

For a few minutes narrow paths slope across the hillside, leading upwards once more. Soon the lighthouse comes into view, but is never quite reached (without a diversion), the path passing beneath it to another lookout post. Here cross a stile and continue ahead with the headland swinging now to the right, and, far away, Criffel and the hazy hills of Galloway easing into view. Ahead, too, across the wide sweep of Saltom Bay, Whitehaven and its suburbs appear, the disfiguring buildings and chimneys of the Marchon chemical works unavoidably drawing the eye.

A lighthouse on St Bees Head was first constructed in 1717, though the present structure, its light more than 100 metres above the sea, was erected in 1866; it is open to visitors, by arrangement.

Finally, the route starts to creep round to the east, the direction of Robin Hood's Bay. At a stile a more prominent path is gained, fenced on the right, and delineated on the left by a sharp drop to a level green pasture suspended halfway down to the seashore. Soon, however, a clifftop path reappears, heading towards Whitehaven until, dramatically, it ends at the very edge of an old quarry, though whether quarrying activity is extinct or on the edge of revival is never quite clear.

Go round the quarry to the end of a lane, near some cottages, and here turn right (waymark and signpost: 'To Sandwith'), following the lane to its meeting with a metalled minor roadway leading, left, down to Sandwith. As the road descends easily to the village, the immense spread of Lakeland fells across the horizon presents a tantalising backdrop – Grasmoor, High Stile, Pillar, Steeple, Red Pike and the Scafells separated by the conspicuous gash of Mickledore.

A convenient bench at the road junction in

Sandwith is temptation enough for a brief respite, especially with the possibility of refreshments nearby, but first-day enthusiasm will soon have feet treading the road again, on through the village, round by the Dog and Partridge, and up to the junction at Lanehead. Cross the minor road (named 'Byerstead Road') and on to a superb green back road leading to Demesne Farm.

> In the distance, a little nearer than the main Lakeland fells, a rounded grassy dome has been looming ever larger. This is Dent Fell, a Lakeland 'hors d'oeuvre', all too soon to be encountered.

At Demesne Farm keep left in front of farm buildings, and then turn right on a farm access track sign-posted: 'Coast to Coast'. Soon the B5345 is reached, and crossed to reach a metalled access track leading down towards Bell House Farm. Keep on past the farm to cross a cattle grid, with a splendid view ahead of Stanley Pond in the foreground and the intricate pattern of fields rising far into the distant folds of flowing fells.

Shortly after the cattle grid take a right fork (waymarked) and descend to a gate, beyond which a less pronounced path descends left (also waymarked), keeping on down the field side to a railway underpass.

> Between Sandwith and Cleator we find ourselves threading a tapestry of patterned fields and flower-decked lanes that try to shrug off the nearby urban influence, and in spring and early summer are sure to have botanists dragging their feet. (Having experienced the walk and its floral richness in its entirety, I feel botanists might well be advised to keep the days short, add an extra week and travel alone, or with very understanding friends!)

Once through the underpass bear half-left across a meadow to a group of trees, and then follow a hedgerow away to a field corner, with Stanley Pond concealed

Moor Row is a small industrial village of grey Victorian terraces that in its heyday was a busy railway meeting point operating passenger and mineral lines; now it is a forlorn reminder of past glories, its working men's club offering the only alcoholic refreshment (if such is needed) until Cleator is reached.

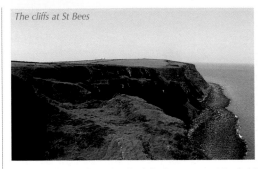

The cliffs at St Bees

nearby. Follow a fence on the left, the corner of the field proving boggy after rain, to a stile adjoining a gate. Keep with the ensuing fence (now on the right) for a while, until the path breaks away to cross the field it borders. More fields follow as the path leads unerringly to another underpass beneath the defunct Cleator Moor to Whitehaven mineral railway. Press on beneath the underpass and ascend easily to a gated access on to the A595 near Scalegill Hall.

Keep ahead across the A595 and head for Moor Row along a metalled roadway.

Follow the road into Moor Row, and at a T-junction, near the post office, turn right, leaving the village and climbing steadily. Shortly, over a brow, a prominent footpath sign on the left locates a few steps up to a stile giving access to a field. Keep ahead with the field boundary, and before long go right into the next field by a stile. Now a succession of stiles and kissing gates take the walk on to Cleator, meeting the edge of the village at its cricket ground from where a metalled roadway leads into the main street.

CLEATOR

Cleator, alas, is like so many of the villages in this part of Lakeland that were dependent on mining for their well-being and prosperity, and has clearly seen better days. The growth of the iron-ore industry, and the rapid building of simple, unattractive terraced houses to meet

the demands of miners, destroyed much of the village's
former charm and character. Affected as it was, Cleator
was not alone in feeling the impact of industrial expan-
sion; other nearby villages – Frizington, Arlecdon and
Cleator Moor – also grew, as between 1840 and 1880
they bore the weight of an increase in population from
835 to 17,651, with the number of miners rising from
60 to over 6,000. These mere statistics, largely derived
from census returns, however, tell little of the real story
that afflicted this proud and beautiful region, a story of
social problems like overcrowding and deprivation, of
hard men, drinking men, who brought to West
Cumberland, be it from Ireland, Scotland, Cornwall,
Northumberland, Lancashire and Yorkshire, a social
atmosphere more akin to the Klondike days that were
yet to beset North America than the north of England.

Now all that remains to delay passers-by is Cleator's
church, dedicated to St Leonard, built from red sandstone. Though modern in style the church has elements
of Norman handiwork in its chancel walls, and one of
the windows depicts the Lady of Egremont and her
husband meeting (St) Bega at the castle gate.

Unlikely to feature high on tourist itineraries (and is
that such a bad thing?), Cleator is nevertheless very
much a gateway to Lakeland; nearby flows the River
Ehen, and that, before long, marks the boundary of the
Lake District National Park.

Cleator to Ennerdale Bridge

Distance: 8.5 kilometres (5.3 miles)
Ascent: 425 metres (1395 feet)

*The walk hastens to leave Cleator behind, and between
its sad reminder of times gone by and the approaches to
the lake at Ennerdale it travels a fascinating route that
only a few and the curious will know. The dome of Dent
on a hot day is an unfunny joke, but otherwise is an
excellent little fell of great stature on which to rev up
for things to come. Dent's panorama is one of the finest*

Wainwright once observed that Dent: 'impels the…urge to linger awhile'. It was a masterpiece of understatement; only the fittest of the fit will feel that lingering is anything like an option. Mere mortals will be obliged to remain collapsed in a heap for some time before taking in the wonders of the panorama, one of Satanic vastness, a map laid out, of towns and villages, fields and furrows, blue-swelling sea and misty isles, far off mountains and richly green valleys; while onward beckon the fells.

in Lakeland and its summit a perfect resting place, while beyond lies the quiet valley of Uldale and the secret meeting place of three sparkling, softly murmuring streams. This is Nannycatch Gate, a hidden gem, a sylvan glade beneath the dark frown of Raven Crag that is sure to call you back when the walk is done.

On reaching the main street in Cleator turn left for a short distance, leaving it, right, into Kiln Brow. Descend until a signpost ('Fell Road via Nook Farm') directs you right to the River Ehen and Blackhow Bridge. Cross the bridge and, having made but the briefest of acquaintances with the River Ehen, turn left on the access road leading to Black How Farm. Go left just before the farm buildings, and in a short while take a signposted track, right, for Dent, soon to join a metalled roadway.

Cross the road to a gate (signposted: 'C-to-C'), and take a broad forestry track leading into Black How Plantation. Ascend easily to a signpost indicating a narrow path going left. Follow this for about 40m/yds and then, at another signpost, head once more for the rising slopes of Dent Fell, following a narrow, rising path through young plantations of spruce. The path climbs relentlessly to the west summit, marked by a large cairn and only reached either with a sudden access of energy and determination, or on hands and knees; the main summit lies a short distance further east, and is marked by a derisory and insulting heap of stones.

The short crossing from Dent's 'traditional' (western) summit and

its true summit to the east, marks a moment of transition, a passing from images of coastal scenery to the magnetism of high Lakeland's western fringe. A short, sometimes damp, depression links the two summits, continuing downwards then to a fence (and stile) at a forest boundary. Enter the forest, and press on ahead and down on a narrow, tree-flanked path to a broad forest trail. Head left along the trail for a short distance, soon leaving it, right, at a stile, for a relaxing green path across open pastureland. Before long, however, this turns into a brutal, knee-wrecking descent to the head of Uldale, a quiet Lakeland retreat of immense charm. Beneath the gaze of Raven Crag, the walk follows the valley bottom, alongside Kirk Beck, shortly to arrive at Nannycatch Gate.

In recent times the next stage of the route, alongside Nannycatch Beck, has been closed by the landowner. At the time of writing (March, 2002), this is a variable thing. There is an alternative from Nannycatch Gate, heading east along a right-of-way to Sillathwaite Farm and from there up to the main fell road, where you turn left to rejoin the original route.

At Nannycatch Gate, go over the stile and right to pass through a narrow defile beneath the slopes of Flat Fell, and later, as the valley forks, branch right to work up to the open fell road. Shorter and steeper options take you on to the fell road a little sooner, near Kinniside Stone Circle, for example, while the most prominent way ahead leads first to a minor access road, at which a right turn leads the short distance to the main fell road.

On reaching the fell road, turn left and allow gravity to draw you down to Ennerdale Bridge, bearing right at a junction finally to reach the village, and to renew that earlier brief acquaintance with the River Ehen.

Most walkers will find Ennerdale an appropriate

conclusion to the first day, while those bound for youth hostels have a little distance yet to go before they can put their heads down for the night.

ENNERDALE BRIDGE

Things have changed in Ennerdale Bridge since one traveller described the pub as 'small, dirty, and filled with roaring tipplers' – and that at nine in the morning! The village now sees few visitors, its general inaccessibility ensuring that the throngs don't inadvertently stumble upon it. Thankfully, it remains a quiet farming and forestry retreat, well known and loved by local people, but never likely to figure highly on tourist itineraries.

Ennerdale Bridge
to Black Sail Youth Hostel

Distance: 14.1 kilometres (8.8 miles)
Ascent: 190 metres (625 feet)

The next stage of the walk ventures into the long recess of Ennerdale, along the southern shores of its lake until

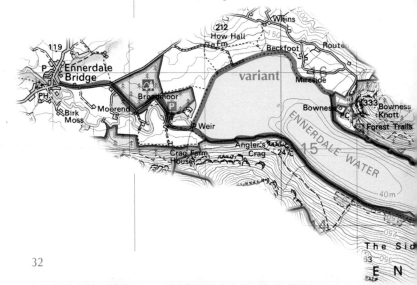

forced to the northern flank for comparatively easy progress to the isolated, but splendidly set, Black Sail Youth Hostel. Most walkers starting from Ennerdale Bridge will find this too short a day, and opt to push on to Seatoller or Rosthwaite. Walkers with relatively little experience of long distance walking may, however, detect the wisdom in electing to inject a couple of short days (the next day, too, to Rosthwaite or Langstrath would be short) into the proceedings at this early stage to allow body and soul to 'acclimatise' instead of slogging onwards remorselessly.

For strong walkers, on a clear day (there is no point in doing it otherwise), there is a fine high level variant from the valley across the summits of the High Stile range, an extravagantly energetic way of getting the blood coursing through the veins. Quite where this variant would end depends entirely on one's level of fitness - Black Sail Youth Hostel, Honister, Seatoller, or, for superhumans only, Rosthwaite - but it is described on pages 39–43, running from Ennerdale Bridge to the top of Honister Pass, where the original route is regained.

Walkers of more modest energies may find the north shore route, well signposted from near the outflow of the lake, an appealing choice, giving as it does rather an earlier view of the great summits at the head of the valley; though these will come soon enough for the rest of us.

Leave Ennerdale Bridge along the minor road for Croasdale, turning right after about 700m/yds to follow a zigzagging road to meet the River Ehen again not far from a North West Water Treatment Works.

By burying most of the actual treatment process underground and building the surface control room in traditional stone and Lakeland green slate, the Treatment Works have the appearance of a small, local farmstead. Water is brought to the works via an 800m long tunnel in which modern pipe-jacking techniques are used to keep surface operations to a minimum; when in full flow it feeds 15 million gallons of water to the new treatment works. When work is complete, the old treatment plant will be demolished and landscaped to provide a small car park and information board for visitors.

continued on page 34

On crossing the River Ehen either elect to go left immediately, following the north shore route to another footbridge leading on to the north shore, from where the line is never in doubt, or continue ahead for a short distance around the water treatment works, and follow a broad track to the lake shore.

The north side is easier walking, but is plagued by day-trippers; the south enjoys rather more in the way of solitude, though many of those day-trippers like to walk all around the lake.

Ennerdale's New Treatment Works forms part of a £12 million scheme to abstract and treat water from Ennerdale for the 60,000 people living in the Copeland Borough area. North West Water acknowledges that Ennerdale and its surroundings is generally recognised

Pillar and Ennerdale

as one of the most beautiful locations in the country, and has gone to great lengths to preserve the environment and the wildlife. For example, the scheme incorporates a specially-designed channel to ensure that migrating salmon and trout can reach the important spawning waters of Ennerdale even during the driest summers.

The sudden impact of Ennerdale's lake as you reach its edge is outstanding, a wonderful and dramatic moment. A good path flirts along its shores, within stepping distance of the water, and continues uneventfull until its encounter with the cliffs of Angler's Crag. Energetic souls may opt for a steeply ascending path, encountered a little before Angler's Crag, crossing the top of the crag, a splendid viewpoint, before descending steeply on the other side. A more pronounced way takes a lower line, and clambers through the fractured base of the crag with much less expenditure of energy.

> A small headland juts out into the lake at this point. This is known as **Robin Hood's Chair**, a fanciful connection, but of interest to Coast to Coasters linking as it does with the final destination, and, for that matter, with his alleged grave on the crossing of Crosby Ravensworth Fell a few days hence.

Once beyond the hiatus of Angler's Crag, the path continues without incident to the head of the lake, following a path sweeping round to join the broad forest trail on the northern side of the valley at Irish Bridge, beneath the minor summit of Latterbarrow and not far from High Gillerthwaite Youth Hostel. The route now follows a simple and direct route, first by metalled roadway and then by forest trail, to a gate leading finally from the forest along the final few strides to Black Sail Youth Hostel. En route, Low Gillerthwaite is encountered, a Field Centre run by Leeds College of Education, and then High Gillerthwaite, a youth hostel. Both these centres, and Black Sail Youth Hostel, are owned by the Forestry Commission.

Above Ennerdale Water is the River Liza, its name thought to have derived from the Icelandic river, Lysá, meaning 'the bright water', and suggestive of the area having been settled by Norsemen. The tumbling waters of the Lisa, half-hidden among ferns and trees, are a bold contrast with the high fells that look down on it.

ENNERDALE

Hitherto glimpsed and suspected, the immensity of the valley head now proclaims itself as first the massive wall, the ridges and green coves of Pillar, and then the bold forms of Kirk Fell and the Gables, Green and Great, begin to dominate the scene.

The chance find, in 1947, of the site of a Neolithic axe factory in Langdale, from which items have been carbon-dated to between 2700 and 2500 BC, and the finding of finished artefacts in Ireland, Scotland and southern England, has led to speculation that Ennerdale, reached via Aaron Slack and Windy Gap (between Great and Green Gable), was the route prehistoric man took to reach the coast.

Much later, the area, especially around upper Ennerdale, was a medieval deer forest under the control of the monks at St Bees, while from 1810 comes the tale of **'T'girt Dog' of Ennerdale**, something of a cross between a mastiff and a greyhound and weighing eight stones. For months it ranged from Cockermouth to Ravenglass, St Bees to Wasdale Head, defying all attempts to capture and kill it, and savaged hundreds of sheep, often wantonly destroying seven or eight sheep in one night before finally it was slain.

Cloaked in forest, once regarded as ugly and unsightly, but now relinquishing its regimented grip under new, more sensitive management, there is no denying the beauty of Ennerdale. Edwin Waugh, a notable Lancashire poet, and at his best when revelling in the wild and stormy side of nature, wrote a most evocative description of the lake in his *Rambles in the Lake Country*. Of a moonlit visit he penned: 'In this sheltered corner little eddies of shimmering silver flit about, – the dainty Ariels of moonlit water; there, is a burnished islet of stirless brilliance, in which even the moon smiles to see herself look so passing fair; and, out beyond, the wide waters are in a tremulous fever of delight with her sweet influence…If there be magic in the world, it is this!'

Nor did Cumberland's own poet, Wordsworth,

neglect the place, remote as it was from his Grasmere home. In *The Brothers* he cast a spell over Ennerdale and the monolith of Pillar Rock, writing:

> 'You see yon precipice; it wears the shape
> Of a vast building made of many crags,
> And in the midst is one particular rock
> That rises like a column from the vale,
> Whence by our shepherds it is called the Pillar.'

Pillar Rock, thankfully you might say, is not on the route, but its presence draws the eye for quite a while as the way ventures deeper and deeper into the valley. Its parent mountain, Pillar, is a 'mighty mass of natural Gothic architecture', a monument to Nature's creation.

Black Sail Youth Hostel to Borrowdale (Rosthwaite)

Distance: 8.8 kilometres (5.5 miles)
Ascent: 340 metres (1115 feet)

Black Sail Youth Hostel lies in one of the most dramatic and awe-inspiring locations in the Lake District, a perfect base for mountain adventurers wanting to cut their teeth on the ring of craggy, challenging summits

Great Gable and Green Gable from Ennerdale

that surround it. Well-established routes leave the youth hostel for the heights, though none of the principal lines is used by this walk, which prefers the crumbly confines of Loft Beck before swinging high across the flanks of Brandreth and Grey Knotts to the top of the Honister Pass.

For walkers thus far sticking with the original line, this is the first moment of real challenge, the first opportunity to come to grips with the mountain uplands of Lakeland, and not a place to linger if the weather is turning for the worse.

On leaving Black Sail Youth Hostel do not be misled by the rather more prominent path heading for a footbridge across the Liza and Black Sail Pass. Instead take a narrow path, becoming clearer, to arrive at the foot of Loft Beck. Cross Loft Beck and begin the steepish pull to the shoulder of fells above. On a warm day the beck is something of a heat trap, but the retrospective views are adequate justification for taking the climb easy.

At the top of Loft Beck a line of cairns directs the path to easier ground, with the summits of Brandreth and Grey Knotts ahead. Gradually the route veers away from these outliers of the Gables as a more prominent path looms ahead. This is Moses' Trod, a long-established trail from Honister to Wasdale and beyond. Away to the left a delightful view of the Buttermere valley opens up, framed between the heights of the High Stile range and Fleetwith Pike.

Moses' Trod, or more correctly, **Moses' Sledgate**, is an old slate road across which Honister slate was transported to Wasdale and out to Ravenglass on the coast; fragments of green Honister slate may still be found along its length. Rather more romantically, it is said to have been named after an illicit whisky distiller who had his still concealed among the surrounding crags. Whether there ever was a still remains uncertain, but there is a theory that Moses was a quarryman at Honister who smuggled plumbago as a sideline, perhaps distilling whisky after his day's work. During the eighteenth century Borrowdale plumbago was very much at a premium, and smuggling likely to have been a profitable business. Either way, the trod serves a useful and convenient purpose for walkers bound for Honister, and the name of Moses, for his sins or otherwise, lives on, remembered by everyone who places foot on Moses' Trod.

Before long the route collides with the Trod at a large cairn, and continues an easy descent northwards to the remains of the tramway and Drum House that served the Dubs Quarry. Here turn right, descending even more steeply for a while to reach the slate quarry buildings at the top of one of Lakeland's better known motor passes, Honister.

The on-going route description for the walk now continues on page 43.

HIGH STILE RANGE AND HAYSTACKS VARIANT:

Ennerdale Bridge to Honister via the High Stile Range and Haystacks.

Distance: 18.5 kilometres (11.5 miles)
Ascent: 1295 metres (4250 feet)

No modest undertaking this, but one that strong walkers capable of handling heavy packs on awkward terrain will find an infinitely more rewarding alternative to the walk through the valley; indeed, walkers stirred by the sight of rugged mountains and with an eye and a soul for the grandness of a setting might well consider dropping back to Ennerdale from Scarth Gap to overnight at the Black Sail Youth Hostel. A somewhat illogical suggestion, this, especially with the youth hostel at Honister within easy reach, but the two locations withstand no comparison – Black Sail wins hands down! – and you can always come back up to Scarth Gap with Haystacks on the morrow.

Various other possibilities plug into the High Stile/Haystacks connection: one uses the valley as far as Black Sail Youth Hostel, and then scampers up to Scarth Gap for the crossing of Haystacks, while the other takes advantage of a break in the forestry near Gillerthwaite to head directly for Red Pike – but why join such a superb ridge in the middle? Better to tackle the whole lot, end to end.

Leave Ennerdale Bridge on the Croasdale road: the objective, Whins Farm (099167). A number of possibilities present themselves: walk along the road; continue to the River Ehen and follow the north shore route until a path leads northwards to the road near the farm; or (the measured route) take the road as if going to the River Ehen, leaving it at the corner of the two plantations (083156) to continue ahead to reach the lake shore. Then follow the shoreline to the path leading up towards Whins Farm.

Great Bourne is the first of the summits along this long ridge, but it is more usually ascended by walkers continuing westwards along the ridge from Red Pike, having dealt with Starling Dodd en route.

From Whins Farm follow the grassy lane directly opposite the road junction to a gate in the intake wall, and there take the path ascending above Gill Beck to the top of the Floutern Pass, a boggy affair, crossed by a fence. Towering above, on the right, is Steel Brow, and the fenceline ascending the fellside steeply should be followed to the summit.

> Ahead now, above the intermediate top of Starling Dodd, Red Pike can be seen in the distance, from this angle quite belying the abruptness of its northern flank. The route lies across Red Pike, mostly on grass and a delight to walk. All around rise majestic peaks Haycock, Steeple, Scoat Fell, Pillar, Kirk Fell and Great Gable on the right, and the Grasmoor range far away to the left.

Leave the grey, rocky top of Great Bourne on a path following a fenceline until the path moves away from it to head for Starling Dodd. Beyond Starling Dodd the path flanks its minor acolyte, Little Dodd, and pursues a dilapidated fenceline, headin for, but not quite reaching, the drop into Ling Comb above Buttermere. As the fenceline bends stay with it until a direct ascent of Red Pike's western slopes may be made.

From Red Pike head initially south and then southeast to follow the rim of the immense corrie embracing Bleaberry Tarn, guided by a continuing line of old fence posts to the highest summit of the range, High Stile. A rather more satisfying line follows the edge of the cliffs (not too closely mind) to cross the top of Chapel Crags.

> Pillar continues to dominate the scene to the south with the summits of the Scafells, the 'Roof of England', peering over its shoulder.

The summit of Red Pike is among the finest in Lakeland for views as here a scene of great beauty unfolds, the ground at your feet dropping severely to reveal the delights of Buttermere far below, while great cirques of lofty mountains frieze the skyline: a dramatic and awe-inspiring prospect. Red Pike also marks a change of terrain as the grassy fells to the west give way to the craggy, cliff-edged summits of High Stile and High Crag. With Red Pike, this magnificent trinity of summits is a masterpiece of natural architecture and an inspiring challenge.

The line of old fence posts which led to High Stile continue now to the next summit, High Crag, though the crags, which here drop into Burtness Combe, do so rather more abruptly than above Chapel Crags.

A loose, steep and (for heavily-laden walkers) awkward descent, southeast, leads first down Gamlin End and then, more or less following an old fence line, through the broken crags and loose scree of a minor top, Seat, before finally gaining more stable ground at Scarth Gap.

> The traverse of the High Stile ridge is one of the finest undertakings in the Lake District, and more than amply repays the effort of slogging up Steel Brow to reach Great Borne; this is not a day to leave cameras anywhere other than at the ready, with the prospect of an untiring succession of majestic views and thrilling situations lying in wait. There is so much to see, so much to capture on film.
>
> From High Crag the onward march across Haystacks has magnetic appeal, precipitous crags on the one hand overlooking Warnscale Bottom and steep green slopes on the other falling back to Ennerdale, while ahead is arrayed a labyrinthine display of knolls and hummocks, shadowy, shallow hollows and bright-eyed tarns through which thread the lines of weaving pathways, curious to explore every corner, reluctant to miss even the slightest change of perspective in what is a lavish wonderland. Haystacks is a mountain for a day to itself: coming as it does as part of an energetic traverse it is all we can do to promise a return.

From the highest point of Scarth Gap ascend a slanting rake, left, to a short downfall of scree, beyond which the path picks a way through a series of minor outcrops to the summit, close by a small tarn.

A twisting path descends from the summit to Innominate Tarn and on, gradually, to the outflow of Blackbeck Tarn before setting off across a boggy col for the steady trek to the remains of Dubs Quarry.

Both Innominate and Blackbeck Tarns are mountain jewels of the highest quality, while an issue of The Gentleman's Magazine, published in 1751, depicted a map of Lakeland with the words 'here eagles build' sprawled across Haystacks, proof, along with nearby Eagle Crag, that eagles did at one time frequent most if not all of the Lakeland valleys.

From Blackbeck Tarn the outflowing waters have carved a deeply incised ravine seemingly with the express purpose of framing a lovely picture of Buttermere, a valley, considered by W.G. Collingwood to be 'as made by Heaven for summer evenings and summer mornings.' Viewed from the portals of Black Beck you can see what he meant.

Beyond Black Beck col a rising path of slate leads to the remains of Dubs Quarry, much in need of preservation. Unerringly, a track leads onwards to its meeting with Moses' Trod, where this variant route rejoins the main line for the descent to the top of Honister Pass, Honister Hause as it is more correctly known.

Walkers with energy to spare after the High Stile traverse (do they exist?), and planning to spend the night at the Honister Youth Hostel, might be tempted by the proximity of Fleetwith Pike, a relatively minor summit, off the main thoroughfare of mountain crossings, but with a stupendous and unrivalled view down the length of Buttermere. The summit may be attained easily from the remains of the Dubs Quarry, and its fine ridge, then followed eastwards to Honister Crag before leaving it to rejoin the main route.

The on-going description for the main line of the walk continues from here.

Honister Quarry is silent now, the cliffs of Honister Crag from which the prized green slate was won echoing only to the sound of walkers' footsteps, whether it will remain that way is another matter.

Working conditions at the quarry were harsh and

Innominate Tarn is, for walkers who over the years have followed the 'Lakeland Fells' gospels according to the late Alfred Wainwright, a place of some poignancy for here were scattered his ashes, as he had wished. It is a place he loved with a great passion, a place he described as 'A lonely spot of haunting charm' – adding: 'If I were destined to drop dead on the fells, this is the place I would like it to happen.' A morbid thought, perhaps, but could we not all think of some place, some time, some company, some circumstance, that we would find most agreeable for our final moments on earth, if we had to?

Innominate Tarn,
Hay Stacks

dangerous. Slate was brought down to the knapping sheds on hurdles, or trail-barrows, which had two inclining handles (stangs) at the front between which the man would position himself, going, like a horse, before the weight. These contraptions weighed as much as eighty pounds empty, and it took the men half an hour of laborious effort to carry them back to the quarries in the honeycomb of tunnels above. The subsequent laden descent, unbelievably, was only a matter of minutes, depending on skill, dexterity and good fortune. Remarkable tales are found of men who worked in the quarries in the nineteenth century: Samuel Trimmer once made fifteen journeys in a day for a bottle of rum and a small percentage of the slate he sledged, and Joseph Clarke of Stonethwaite, who made seventeen journeys, bringing down each time 640 pounds of slate, a total of 10,880 pounds, in one day. 'His greatest day's work,' writes Harriet Martineau, 'was bringing 11,771 pounds; in how many journeys it is not remembered: but in fewer than seventeen.' This highly dangerous method of obtaining slate was ended in 1881, when a gravitational railway was introduced. Quarry worker, like drystone wallers, often lived during the week in small huts on the hillsides, going home only from Saturday night until Monday morning, and while away, communicating with their wives by carrier pigeons.

Now from Honister thoughts turn to Borrowdale, that most loved and most popular of Lakeland's valleys.

From the summit of the pass follow the descending motor road until a former highway, now abandoned, branches off on the left. This was a toll road, and provides a traffic free descent to Seatoller, reaching the tiny village not far from a National Park information centre at Dalehead Barn.

Descend through the village and turn left into the car park, leaving it by a stile at its far end. Keep right at a fork, to follow a pleasant path above the River Derwent to reach Longthwaite Youth Hostel.

[By way of a minor variant you can, at the fork, go left and follow an ascending track, quite broad and rocky underfoot, then climb into woodland through a gate. This is Johnny's Wood, where a conspicuous path leads around a small hillock before descending to cross a fence by a step-stile. Turn right, the path leading to a kissing gate close by the youth hostel. At the end of the wall before the youth hostel turn left and ascend a short grassy path to an access road: the main route is rejoined at this point.]

Go through a gate and over a humped-back bridge spanning the River Derwent to enter Rosthwaite.

Follow the road beyond for a short distance to a bridge and then turn left at a footpath sign. Continue past a number of small cottages and through another gate to enter a pasture of low scrub, following a fence and then a wall to a gate. Once through the gate turn right to a metalled road, and then left to follow the road round until the main road through the valley is reached; the village centre lies just to the right.

BORROWDALE

Borrowdale lies at the very heart of Lakeland, its great length probing far into the 'turbulent chaos of mountain behind mountain, rolled in confusion' that greeted Thomas Gray when, the day after his arrival at Keswick on 2 October 1769, he 'rose at seven, and walked out under the conduct of [his] landlord to Borrowdale.' It is

Rosthwaite is a small, peaceful community flanking the roadside. Unwittingly, Sir Hugh Walpole, has, however, planted the seeds of discord, for at least three houses claim to be the 'original' of Rogue Herries' Farm. At a more prosaic level, it is a fine end to a day that might have started far away at Ennerdale Bridge, a good spot to prepare for the next day, and '…a rare chance to sleep in Arcadia.'

the most beautiful of valleys, a tangled landscape of craggy precipices, richly verdant woodlands, vivid green pastures fed by sparkling rivers and streams, white cottages and rustic farm buildings, all in a setting of Nature's own perfection. Journalist Bernard Levin once observed (during his trek in *Hannibal's Footsteps*) that any 'varied landscape, provided it is not marred by hideous…man-made objects…is beautiful', commenting how this suggested that 'the harmonies of nature are so powerful that no matter what instruments they are played on, in what combinations and at what relative strengths, the result will be pleasing.' He noted, too, that 'if the man-made objects…are not ugly and do blend well…nature absorbs them into the picture and they actually enhance its beauty.' Nowhere is that perception better exemplified than in Borrowdale. Sadly, the walk's acquaintance with these Elysian fields is woefully brief; no sooner does it enter Borrowdale than it departs into the cleavage of the Stonethwaite valley.

Borrowdale (Rosthwaite) to Grasmere (Goody Bridge) via Far Easedale

Distance: 11.3 kilometres (7 miles)
Ascent: 535 metres (1755 feet)

The section of the walk between Rosthwaite and Patterdale can be accomplished in one day, though it would be better with an overnight halt at or near Grasmere. Speed of progress is the obvious, and only, tolerable reason for pushing across in one day, while a more leisurely approach permits at the very least a high level excursion on the second day over the great heights of the Helvellyn range. Whatever choice you make, beauty, in all its guises, is sustained throughout.

If electing to stay in Grasmere, a fine variant makes use of the long ridge leading to Helm Crag, descending from there to the village. This is detailed on pages 49–50.

Walkers not staying in Grasmere, and wanting to avoid it altogether, can continue from Greenup Edge, either directly into Wyth Burn aiming for the southern edge of Thirlmere and then ascending Dunmail Raise to follow Raise Beck to Grisedale Tarn, or continue to the head of Far Easedale, there to swing out along the high ground to Steel Fell, high above Dunmail Raise, from where a very steep descent may be made to the top of the pass. Both of these options can be physically demanding, especially after prolonged wet weather.

Leave Rosthwaite as if heading for Keswick, but in only a few strides turn right at the entrance to Hazelbank Hotel on a public bridleway (signposted: 'Stonethwaite' and 'Watendlath'). The path leads to an arched foot-bridge spanning Stonethwaite Beck, beyond which turn right on a signposted footpath to Stonethwaite. An inter-mittently enclosed path now runs alongside the beck for a while, later becoming a field path leading to Stonethwaite Bridge.

> From the high point of the path the view ahead to Eagle Crag opens up, while to the right may be picked out the summits of Base Brown, Green Gable and Lingmell, the latter rising directly behind the great white mare's tail of Taylorgill Frice.

In Far Easedale

47

At Stonethwaite Bridge the path continues ahead (signposted: 'Grasmere via Greenup Edge') to the source of Stonethwaite Beck, lavish product of Greenup Gill and Langstrath Beck.

Cascades here form delightful company, notably Galleny Force just below the confluence, while the encompassing scenery is so extravagantly beautiful and inspiring you could almost believe nature is showing off! This is Lakeland at its best.

With the show of cascades beyond the dark frown of Eagle Crag increasing with every step, the landscape becomes more austere as Greenup Edge is approached. As the sound of waterfalls is left behind, the path springs upon an unsuspected corrie, a vast green bowl high in the hills, beneath the summit of High Raise. Nearby

En route a memorial plaque affixed to a boulder commemorates a walker who 'died in peace under the shelter of this rock in the early hours of Sunday 8th January 1939.' Did he choose his time and place, I wonder?

Lining Crag stands sentinel over this lonely spot, and is approached on an ascending path, and then passed on a restored footpath which must have shed a gallon or two of perspiration in the making.

Once above Lining Crag most of the uphill work is done, a cairned path leading across frequently boggy ground to traverse Greenup Edge to the head of Wyth Burn. A descending path now traverses a boggy shelf to meet the grassy col of Far Easedale Head at a redundant stile.

The ensuing descent into Far Easedale, although the

48

main route, need only be followed if time is of the essence or in bad weather. The route is never in doubt, a rough and pleasant walk largely in the company of Far Easedale Gill, leading to the outskirts of Grasmere at Goody Bridge.

The on-going route description for the walk continues on page 50.

GIBSON KNOTT AND HELM CRAG VARIANT

Borrowdale (Rosthwaite) to Grasmere (Goody Bridge) via Gibson Knott and Helm Crag

Distance: 12.1 kilometres (7.6 miles)
Ascent: 600 metres (1970 feet)

Only walkers in a hurry top reach Grasmere will follow the main line down Far Easedale, especially when a significantly better alternative is available in the form of the long ridge on the north side of the valley, passing over Gibson Knott to the summit of Helm Crag.

Follow the route to Far Easedale Head from where a prominent, narrow path runs out to pass first round Calf Crag before continuing in entertaining fashion to Gibson Knott and, beyond the dip to Bracken Hause, a final steep flourish to the chaotic topknot of Helm Crag.

Though never in question, the path does not always visit the various minor summits, but simply presses on its determined and enterprising way, keen to gaze down on the beauty that is the Vale of Grasmere.

The summit rocks of *Helm Crag* are an amazing array of pinnacles and tilted rock slabs, many of which over the years have attracted names; indeed, Helm Crag is probably, visually at least, the best known of all the Lakeland summits, instantly identified by everyone who continues north from Grasmere bound for Dunmail Raise. One of its formations, viewed from the vicinity of Grasmere, is immediately recognisable and universally known as the Lion and the Lamb, truly one of the most distinguished of Lakeland tops. Also named is the summit rock itself, known, for obvious reasons when seen at close quarters, as the Howitzer; I would encourage anyone who wants to claim to have 'conquered' Helm Crag at least to touch its very top, but to discourage everyone, including the most hare-brained, from actually attempting to stand on it!

Much less obvious when standing next to them, the Lion and the Lamb are passed by as the summit is left. After a certain amount of twisting and turning on the descending path the valley bottom is reached, and the relaxing road out followed sedately as far as Goody Bridge, where the onward route branches left.

The on-going route description for the walk continues from here.

Walkers continuing to Grasmere should simply follow the road ahead from Goody Bridge, entering the village centre directly.

GRASMERE

Approaching from Dunmail Raise, Thomas Gray wrote of Grasmere: 'The bosom of the mountains, spreading here into a broad bason, discover in the midst of Grasmere-water; its margin is hollowed into small bays with iminences; some of rock, some of soft turf, that half conceal and vary the figure of the little lake they command...a little unsuspected Paradise.' Thirty years later it was William Wordsworth who came this way, concluding that one day this place 'Must be his home, this valley be his world...'.

The attractions of Grasmere are still many, as are the tourists that in summer flock to the village on their respective quests. Valiantly, the village struggles to retain its dignity and charm above the rising tide of visitors, teased in by holiday brochures and coach tour operators to find pleasure and enjoyment in crowded streets, amid jostling throngs, and souvenirs galore. Only in winter, when the last of the day-trippers has gone, does any semblance return of how life might have seemed in Gray's and Wordsworth's time, the still pall of wood smoke lying frozen above an ice-held lake, sunlight chiming through icy, crystal fingers, black ravens winging businesslike above the bracken brown fells.

Grasmere (Goody Bridge) to Patterdale (Grisedale Bridge)

Distance: 11.1 kilometres (7 miles)
Ascent: 505 metres (1655 feet)

Walkers who stayed overnight in Grasmere will need to retreat the short distance to Goody Bridge to resume the journey eastwards from the point at which it was left. It is perfectly feasible simply to walk up to the main road, but the quiet back road from Goody Bridge has much charm and provides a fine prospect of the onward route.

Between Grasmere and Patterdale there is little to tax walkers who have accomplished the crossing thus far without difficulty; a simple high level mountain pass lies in wait beyond which a long and invigorating descent leads to the valley of Patterdale. By way, therefore, of variant fare, two high level possibilities are on hand, though neither should be contemplated in poor visibility or other adverse weather conditions. One, involving a fair bit of effort, climbs north to traverse the long ridge to Helvellyn, followed by the delights of

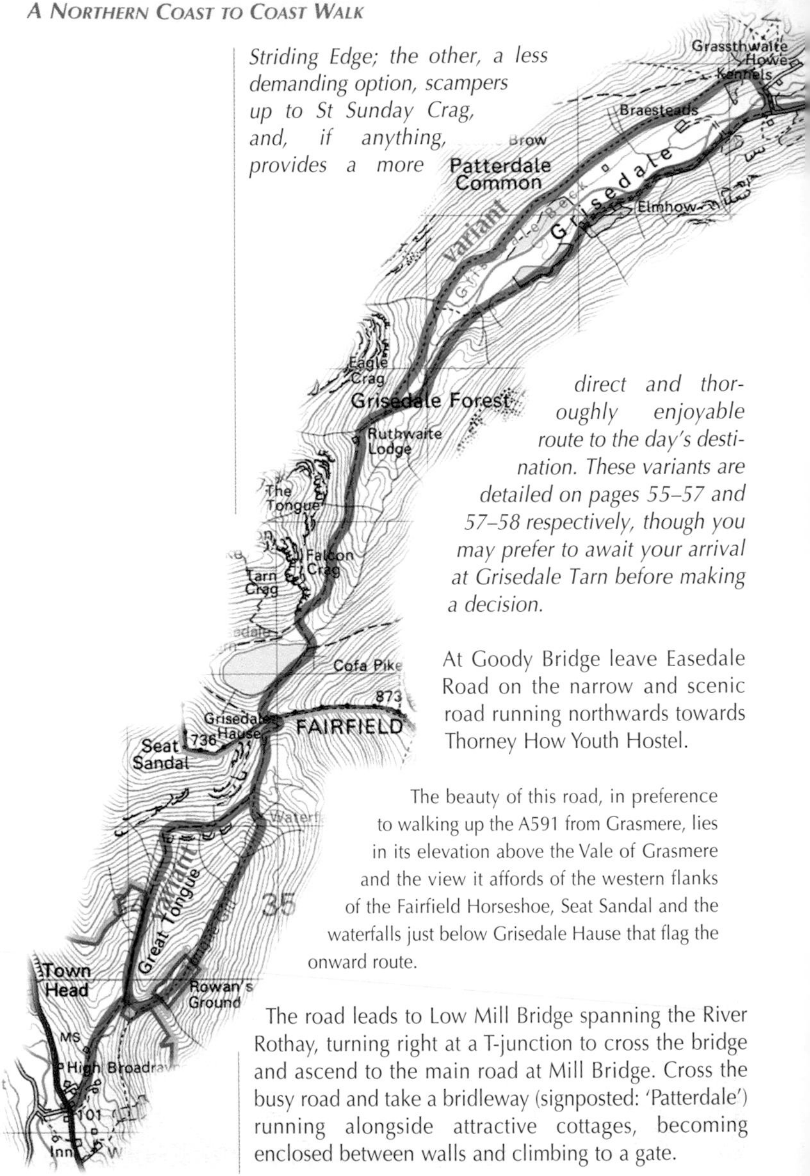

Striding Edge; the other, a less demanding option, scampers up to St Sunday Crag, and, if anything, provides a more

Grassthwaite Howe

Kennfels

Braesteads

Brow

Patterdale Common

Variant

Grisedale

Elmhow

Eagle Crag

Grisedale Forest

Ruthwaite Lodge

The Tongue

Falcon Crag

Tarn Crag

Cofa Pike

873

Grisedale Hause

FAIRFIELD

Seat Sandal 736

Water

Great Tongue

35

Town Head

Rowan's Ground

MS

High Broadra

101

Inn

direct and thoroughly enjoyable route to the day's destination. These variants are detailed on pages 55–57 and 57–58 respectively, though you may prefer to await your arrival at Grisedale Tarn before making a decision.

At Goody Bridge leave Easedale Road on the narrow and scenic road running northwards towards Thorney How Youth Hostel.

The beauty of this road, in preference to walking up the A591 from Grasmere, lies in its elevation above the Vale of Grasmere and the view it affords of the western flanks of the Fairfield Horseshoe, Seat Sandal and the waterfalls just below Grisedale Hause that flag the onward route.

The road leads to Low Mill Bridge spanning the River Rothay, turning right at a T-junction to cross the bridge and ascend to the main road at Mill Bridge. Cross the busy road and take a bridleway (signposted: 'Patterdale') running alongside attractive cottages, becoming enclosed between walls and climbing to a gate.

Beyond the gate the path continues to climb for a while, then levels as it approaches a group of sheep enclosures at the tip of Great Tongue. Two possibilities here present themselves: one to take a path climbing left, via Little Tongue Gill; the other opting for a path going right, across Tongue Gill.

The green path of Little Tongue Gill is a route by which Victorian visitors would travel on ponies to the summit of Helvellyn; this climbs rather tediously until it levels to cross the flank of Seat Sandal. The ascent by Tongue Gill is much more entertaining: it crosses Little Tongue Gill first, by a footbridge or a ford, and then Tongue Gill itself, rising in easy stages. Gradually the path approaches the waterfalls near the head of the gill and arrives at a rock step, climbed by a series of ledges and a rough path.

Cross the stream ahead, and climb over rough ground to a false col beyond which lies a shallow hollow, giving the impression that it might once have held a lake. Continue rockily around its left edge and climb easily to Grisedale Hause.

At **Grisedale Hause** a vastly different prospect opens up. Hitherto the views have all been retrospective: now it is

Grisedale Tarn

There is a legend about Grisedale Tarn that into it Duvenald (corrupted to Dunmail) King of Strathclyde, of which north Cumbria was a part, cast his crown, ceremoniously rejecting his insignia of royalty before taking to the pilgrim's staff. Some claim that Dunmail lies buried, slain by Saxons, beneath the cairn at the head of the nearby pass that bears his name; alas, reality, as ever, destroys the myth, for it is known he died peacefully in bed in Rome. Around this legend Graham Sutton, author of a number of novels about Lakeland, spun a chilling short story entitled Dusk below Helvellyn.

time to look forward across the great bowl that houses Grisedale Tarn to what lies ahead as slowly (there is no hurry just yet!) we start to leave behind the great rugged heights of central Lakeland to head for the sublime traverse of limestone country and the dales of Yorkshire.

Grisedale Tarn is an ideal place for a pause, deep set beneath the hillsides of Dollywaggon Pike, Fairfield and Seat Sandal, a setting wild and grand with a true mountain atmosphere, though none of the surrounding heights presents its best profile to the lonely lake. T.S. Tschiffeley in his Bridle Paths through England said Grisedale Tarn 'brought back memories of the highlands of Bolivia and Peru' – perhaps it did, for it is a fine jewel in a fine crown, on a still evening faithfully mirroring the surrounding hills.

From the hause descend a stony path to cross the outflow of the tarn and traverse half left to begin the descent into the long reaches of Grisedale.

Walkers taking one of the variant routes will leave the main line at this point.

A number of paths lead away from the outflow of the tarn to a large cairn at the start of the descent. Make for this and then pursue the downward trail, rocky underfoot but never in doubt, as far as the ruins of Ruthwaite Lodge.

After only a few minutes' descent it is possible to deviate, right, for a moment to visit 'Brothers Parting', where one of Wordsworth's poems (all but illegible now) is carved in a rock tablet, commemorating the parting of Wordsworth from his brother John, Captain of the Earl of Abergavenny, in which he perished in 1805.

Press on beyond the Lodge, descending a little abruptly for a while until the path forks. Either path will now take you to Grisedale. That on the right is a speedier route down the valley, but suffers from the gloom cast upon it by the towering bulk of St Sunday Crag.

By going left at the fork and across a wooden

bridge, however, a more satisfying descent may be made keeping to the north side of the valley, twisting and turning, and undulating from time to time until finally the path meets that descending (on the left) from Striding Edge, at a gate. Go right, through the gate, dropping across a sloping pasture to another gate beyond which an access track leads to a bridge spanning Grisedale Beck, where it rejoins the alternative route left earlier.

Here a metalled road is reached, and followed easily to the A592 at Grisedale Beck. Part way down this road a gate on the right marks a minor variant finish to Patterdale village through the delightful Glenamara Park.

The on-going description for the walk from Patterdale continues on page 59.

The on-going description for the walk from Patterdale continues on page 59.

Variants: *The following two variants offer alternative ways of reaching Patterdale from Grisedale Tarn. The first takes in Helvellyn and the long ridge of Striding Edge; this is initially strenuous and then demands exceptional care by walkers with heavy packs in the descent to, and subsequently crossing of, Striding Edge. This variant should be considered only by exceptionally strong walkers, travelling in good weather conditions; if either criterion is not satisfied, opt for the Grisedale valley.*

The second variant poses no such carrying problems, and rises easily from Grisedale Tarn to the summit of St Sunday Crag, dropping then over a minor summit, Birks, before reaching Patterdale.

HELVELLYN VARIANT

Grasmere (Goody Bridge) to Patterdale (Grisedale Bridge) via Helvellyn and Striding Edge

Distance: 14.5 kilometres (9 miles)
Ascent: 1010 metres (3315 feet),
plus a nominal ascent along Striding Edge

Pursue the route described above between Goody

Bridge and Grisedale Tarn outflow, and from there ascend the arid scree path climbing in a series of zigzags to the broad path below the summit of Dollywaggon Pike.

> This is a tiresome and wearying treadmill, and not a promising start to the variant, but once easier ground is reached all troubles are soon forgotten, as legs swing free, and wide-ranging views seem to lighten the load.
>
> Like Nethermost Pike, shortly to be encountered, Dollywaggon Pike is an excellent vantage point, and neither summit should, given the effort expended in getting this far, be avoided.

Leave this path for the summit, following the cliff edge to the summit cairn. Dollywaggon has a second summit nearby which likewise may be reached along the rim of cliffs. By continuing in parallel with, but not too close to, the cliffs, High Crag is next reached, soon followed by the spacious summit plateau of Nethermost Pike, adorned by two cairns.

> Beyond Nethermost Pike the path descends to a shallow col, Swallow Scarth (343145) not named on 1:50,000 map) from where a blazed trail leads to the summit of Helvellyn.

Retreating from the summit, a stone, cross-shaped shelter is regained from which a path skirts the rim of the corrie above Red Tarn to a large stone memorial.

> This moving memorial commemorates a loyal dog's vigil, for at the foot of these precipitous slopes Charles Gough of Manchester perished in 1805, his body watched over by his dog for three months:

> Not yet quite deserted, though lonely extended,
> For, faithful in death, his mute favourite attended,
> The much-loved remains of her defended,
> And chased the hill-fox and the ravens away.
> (Walter Scott: 1771–1832)

> Wordsworth, too, wrote of this sad event, while in

present times Richard Adams alluded to it in his book *The Plague Dogs*, inspired, no doubt, by such canine fidelity.

Not far beyond the memorial begins the broken and slippery descent to the foot of Striding Edge, and great care is needed here.

The Edge looks fearfully intimidating, especially viewed from above, when the crest appears forbiddingly narrow and its flanks long and steep; yet its dangers are much less real, and a cool head and steady foot will soon hasten its traverse.

On reaching the narrow col linking Helvellyn to Striding Edge, move slightly right to clamber up a rocky gully, and so begin the long traverse of the ridge, a fine, airy prospect, with no real doubt about the onward route.

Many nineteenth-century writers regarded **Striding Edge** with a degree of terror, considered by Harriet Martineau as 'absolutely precipitous on each side, and the top of the rocky wall was not more than from one or two yards wide, whilst in some places we could not see, before we came to it, as much ground as would serve to plant a foot upon – the rocks presenting their sharp and rugged edges upwards, like slates or tiles standing on end.'

Gradually the ruggedness of Striding Edge ebbs away as a path leads to the Hole in the Wall. A little more broken pathwork and then the long descending route to the Grisedale valley lies ahead, child's play by comparison. At a gate descend a sloping pasture to another gate, and shortly a bridge over Grisedale Beck, where the valley line is rejoined at a metalled roadway dropping to Grisedale Bridge.

Walkers following this variant should now refer to page 59 for the on-going route from Patterdale.

Cloaked as it was in a mantle of exaggerated dangers, it was inevitable that Striding Edge would find its way into a novel or two. Miss Braddon, author of Phantom Fortune, commented: 'A mountain in the abstract is not a place for human peregrination. Sheep appear to like it, but that is their affair; and the fact that they are better as mutton in consequence makes one indulgent to their absurdity; but that humanity should ever be yearning to explore regions in which it has to sprawl and cling and clamber like a fly on a ceiling, is surely a subject for mild wonder.' She did add: 'The Striding Edge is chic.'

Looking back into Grisedale

ST SUNDAY CRAG VARIANT

Grasmere (Goody Bridge) to Patterdale (Grisedale Bridge) via St Sunday Crag

Distance: 11.5 kilometres (7.2 miles)
Ascent: 840 metres (2755 feet)

The variant across St Sunday Crag is considerably easier than over Helvellyn and Striding Edge, and makes a fine, high level traverse without too much expenditure of energy.

Once again the route to Grisedale Tarn is as before. From there look for a narrow path ascending obliquely across the lower slopes of Fairfield and Cofa Pike to an obvious depression on the skyline, Deepdale Hause. From the hause continue northeastwards on a broad path following the highest ground to the summit of St Sunday Crag.

A path leaves the triangular plateau that is St Sunday Crag's summit heading northeast for the minor peak, Birks. In places a little steep, the path is, however, never in doubt, and drops to a grassy col from which a diversion will lead to the top of Birks.

Return to the path (if you visited the summit) and descend to Thornhow End before taking a path going left to the Grisedale valley route (the measured line), or right, to approach Patterdale village direct through Glenamara Park (a slightly shorter option).

The on-going description for the main line of the walk continues from here.

PATTERDALE

The dale that we today call Patterdale is named after St Patrick, one of three famous missionaries (the others were St Ninian and St Kentigern) thought to have travelled in this region on evangelical missions during the early years of the fifth century. Little is clear about the growth of Christianity at this time, for this was a troubled era; the Roman Empire, preoccupied with problems at home, was withdrawing all Roman units from its Cumbrian forts, and an intense period of tribal strife was to follow.

Patrick, thought to have been born in the Solway region around the year 389, was reared in the Christian faith. At the age of sixteen he had the misfortune, along with 'male and female slaves of his father's house' to be captured by Irish pirates. He was taken to Ireland where he was obliged to work as a cattle herder. During his time in captivity his faith deepened until, after six years of slavery, he experienced visions and heard angelic voices urging him to return to his own country to spread the word of Christ, a calling which on his escape and return to England he dutifully obeyed, travelling far into the mountains to convert the natives. Patterdale, St Patrick's Dale, is known to have been an area of a well-established, if scattered, British settlement, and an obvious target for the young man's task, though there remains even today a strongly held view that he never came near the place!

The modern village, described in Baddeley's *Guide to the English Lake District* as 'one of the most charmingly situated in Britain, and in itself clean and comely', lies at the southern end of Ullswater. Unspoiled by the livelier atmosphere that draws non walking day-trippers to nearby Glenridding, Patterdale maintains a serene aloofness, content to cater for those who come to enjoy the relative peace and quiet of its surroundings. Little has changed here over the years; encircled by rugged heights, and with the beauty of arguably Lakeland's

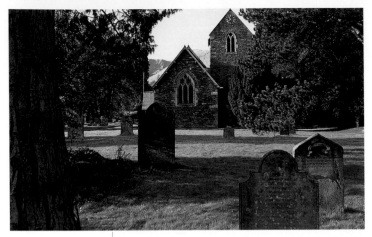

Patterdale Church

finest lake close by, the village pursues life placidly, keeping sacrosanct its typical Lakeland characteristics. One such characteristic, as Frank Singleton put it, is that it 'establishes a great hold on the affections of those who visit it…there is everything here from the silence of the lake and the lonely places among the hills to the busy humanity of the village.'

Many of these remote villages were often presided over by one family; in Patterdale it was the Mounseys, described as the 'kings' of Patterdale, who lived at Patterdale Hall, now extensively rebuilt, but dating from around 1677. Even among such local 'royalty' all was not all sweetness and light however, for Dorothy Wordsworth, in her Journal for the 21st December 1801 gives a little insight into life at Patterdale Hall, writing: 'When we were at Thomas Ashburner's on Sunday Peggy talked about the Queen of Patterdale. She had been brought to drinking by her husband's unkindness and avarice. She was formerly a very nice tidy woman. She had taken to drinking but that was better than if she had taken to something worse (by this I suppose she meant killing herself). She said that her husband used to be out all night with other women and she used to hear him come in, in the morning, for they never slept together…'

Patterdale
(Grisedale Bridge) to Shap

Distance: 24 kilometres (15 miles)
Ascent: 995 metres (3265 feet)

The great upland mass of the High Street range stands between Patterdale and the end of the next day at Shap, a kind of 'sleeping policeman' before the Lake District finally releases its hold and allows the walk to head for Yorkshire. Obligingly, this section puts all the hard work into the first half, allowing a less demanding conclusion in which to appreciate the gradual change of scenery that heralds the approach to Shap and the margins of limestone country. Walkers reluctant to surrender the heights until the very last moment may take a variant line between The Knott (Rampsgill Head) and Burnbanks, northwards along the High Raise ridge, adding nothing to the overall distance and little to the ascent. A rather more energetic second half can be found over the Gatescarth Pass and into Wet Sleddale: these options are detailed on pages 74–75 and 75–76 respectively.

Walkers reaching Patterdale at Grisedale Bridge should turn right along the road and pass by the church to reach a broad track on the left, alongside the George Starkey Memorial Hut. The track is signposted 'Howtown' and 'Boredale', and leads to a bridge spanning Goldrill Beck, beyond which it continues to Side Farm (Camping). Once past the farm turn right on a broad path (slate signpost: 'Angle Tarn' and 'Boredale Hause') and start to climb a little, heading for the scattered farm buildings and cottages of Rooking.

Walkers who entered Patterdale through Glenamara Park and Mill Moss should leave the village by the side road just south of the White Lion Hotel, swinging round left to end at a corner, meeting the above route at a gate giving access to the open fell.

The path now climbs steeply, right, for a short while to a fork. Both the ensuing paths lead with minimal effort to Boredale Hause, with nothing to choose between them, except that the left fork leads to an old iron bench (dated 1897) from which (only for a moment) to take in the green loveliness of the valley below and the rugged heights just traversed, of Striding Edge and Helvellyn, Nethermost Pike and Dollywaggon Pike. As the route approaches Boredale Hause this view, by no means yet finished with, is particularly outstanding.

Overlooked by the broad spread of nearby Place Fell, Boredale Hause shelters the remains of a chapel, these days looking very much like a ruined sheepfold. As the Hause is reached, two collapsed cairns are encountered on a short stretch of level ground. Nearby, cross a small beck, right, onto a prominent path. By a series of twists, turns and undulations, the path works in and out of hollows and around grassy hillocks until, as Angle Tarn Pikes first come into view, there is a splendid framed view down to Brotherswater and beyond to the sinuous line of Kirkstone Pass. The path continues easily, passes beneath Angle Tarn Pikes, and then rounds a corner to spring dramatically upon Angle Tarn itself. Away to the right the great spread of the Fairfield and Helvellyn massifs sweeps round in a craggy arc.

The path descends easily to the tarn, following its edge to climb again with ever-increasing views westwards to a level stretch of ground approaching Satura Crag. (Thornthwaite Crag is the conspicuous summit directly ahead, viewed end on.) Go through a gate and pass beneath Satura Crag, where the broad expanse of the fells still to be climbed rolls across the horizon. Beyond Satura Crag, muddy ground and an undulating path crossing Prison Gill and Sulphury Gill, lead to the final ascent to The Knott, merging with a path ascending from Hartsop and Hayeswater just below the summit at a wall corner.

In good visibility it is a simple and rewarding prospect to cross the top of Rampsgill Head before heading for Kidsty Pike. This minor deviation would rob Kidsty Pike of the distinction of being the highest point crossed by the main line of the walk, but provides a stunning view northwards down the length of Ramps Gill.

Walkers wanting to take the high level variant between The Knott and Burnbanks should now refer to pages 74–76.

continued on page 64

Cairn

Dod

Waterfall

Measand End

Lad Crags

Laythwaite Crags

Whelter Bottom

Benty Howe

Whelter Crags

HAWESWATER RESERVOIR

Rampsgill Head

Randale Beck

Birks Crag

Kidsty Pike

Kidsty Howes

Riggindale

Short Stile

Riggindale Beck

Riggindale Crag

In less than ideal visibility stay with the path passing round The Knott (a slight diversion is needed if you want to add the summit to the walk) and continue towards a depression known as the Straits of Riggindale. Just before the lowest point is reached turn abruptly left on a good path skirting the rim of the steep drop to Riggindale.

63

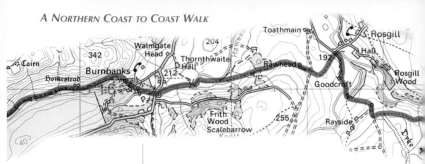

This is a fascinating spot: bold in its architecture, with sweeping Arcadian fellsides dropping to the valley below, the arrow-straight thrust of Rough Crag on the right apposed by Kidsty Pike's flanks of crag and scree. Across this narrow strait the Roman legions threaded their 'High Street'. Their loftiest highway in the country, reaching almost 830 metres (2700 feet) on the whaleback summit that now bears its name. The road linked forts at Galava, Ambleside, and Brocavum (Brougham) at the confluence of the Lowther and Eamont rivers, built, it has been suggested, to prevent the people of Hartsop, Deepdale, Glencoyndale and Bannerdale from joining forces with the tribesmen in Mardale, Bampton and Askham to attack the fort at Brougham. Whether that is so remains unclear; indeed there is some doubt the Romans were even the original route-finders. A Langdale axe found near

Patterdale

Troutbeck suggests a prehistoric route across the mountains to the Neolithic and Bronze Age settlements among the limestone hills of east Westmorland. If that is true, the route was pioneered more than two thousand years before the Romans. Whatever the truth, the Roman 'High Street' remains as a lasting memorial to the skill and endurance of the Roman engineers and 'navvies' who, far from the comforts of home, built and patrolled it in all weathers.

The path curves uneventfully above Riggindale to the sharp summit of Kidsty Pike, a profile recognisable from as far away as the M6 motorway, but on closer inspection a sham in terms of independent grandeur as a mountain, for in reality it is no more than a bump on the shoulder of Rampsgill Head. No such falsehood for its setting however: nothing could be finer, a perfect place to rest awhile after the exertions of the pull from Patterdale.

Silent and observant walkers may be privileged to spot

Angle Tarn

Looking back to Patterdale on the ascent to Boredale Hause

here some of the deer that roam freely upwards across the fells from their sanctuary in Martindale, or the hardy half-wild fell ponies that wander through even the most bitter of winters. Rough fell sheep scrounge scraps of food and nuzzle into your sac (if you let them), and, from time to time, the lone, furtive shape of a fox skulks along beneath the crags. Most thrilling of all, however, is the effortless flight of Lakeland's golden eagles that returned to this region after an absence lasting more than one and a half centuries.

Descend the long east ridge of Kidsty Pike: the going is simple, and the line more distinct now than of old. After a brief skirmish with the rocky upthrust of Kidsty Howes the walk drops swiftly to the shores of Haweswater, reaching the reservoir near the site of Riggindale Farm, a casualty of the flooding of the valley in the 1930s.

Walkers bound for Burnbanks should go left at the foot of the ridge, across the bridge spanning Randale Beck, and then down the entire length of Haweswater on a clear path throughout, until Burnbanks is reached. Walkers taking the Wet Sleddale option must go right following a conspicuous path to cross The Rigg, and keeping above the woodland to Mardale Head.

> There is little along the walk to Burnbanks to detract from the pervading air of calm: a quiet, restful interlude, a time for reflecting on footsteps past, an oasis in the rigours of a long walk where we may replenish our spiritual as well as physical reserves, plodding on peaceably.
>
> **Haweswater**, once of modest proportions, was in the 1930s enlarge to provide water for the thirsts of Manchester, and with it ended an era, for the building of the dam brought the demise of a number of valley farmsteads, and of Mardale itself, a tiny village with its legendary Dun Bull Inn that few now will recall visiting. Passage of time has refashioned the harsh lines of man's intrusions, though drought conditions still lay bare the skeletal remains of the village where visitors with vulturine instincts plunder the walls and buildings for souvenirs that would be far better left to rest in peace.

It was from the slopes of Rough Crag that I first came eye to eye, literally, with a golden eagle, as it slid lazily by less than fifty feet away. Wondering whether eagles ever looked on writers as an alfresco snack I lay motionless, totally in awe of its supreme mastery of the air. The moment was an experience that was long to remain alive in my memory, until, many years later in the Pyrenees, I was rather too closely 'surveyed' by a griffon vulture.

Haweswater

Of Haweswater, Baddeley, who in an early edition of his renowned guide described the Dun Bull Inn as having 'lately been enlarged and now offers very fair accommodation', later claims 'There is no aping of the grandeur of Windermere, the loveliness of Derwentwater, or the wildness of Wastwater, but – although it is a reservoir and somewhat artificial – not to have seen Haweswater would have been to fall short of a just appreciation of the beauties of English Lakeland.'

Along the northwest shore of Birks Crag is the site of an ancient British fort, while the falls of Measand Beck, known as The Forces, offer a moment's pause. In its original state, before the waterworks activities, the hanging valley of Fordingdale (not named on the 1:50000 map), through which Measand Beck flows, ended in a massive fan of gravel and boulders spreading so far out it almost severed the lake.

Just after Measand Beck a last opportunity arises to take in the great sweep of mountains at the head of the valley, a final, final look at a landscape that has set a high standard for the rest of the journey to follow. That the standard is maintained, in very different ways, is a tribute to our northern English heritage.

Across Haweswater the wooded slopes of Naddle Forest rise sharply to a rounded lump known as Hugh's Laithes Pike. A minor summit crowned by a large stone, the top is said to mark the last resting place of Jimmie Lowther, who after a riotous life contrived to break his neck steeplechasing while drunk. Having died too suddenly for a death's-door repentance Jimmie could find no rest in his grave, and in spite of all the parson's efforts to lay his ghost, continued to trouble the villagers. Finally, weary of Jimmie's hauntings, the villagers dug up his body and re-buried it on the highest point of

Naddle Forest where he would bother them no longer. For all we know, he's still up there, haunting the occasional passer-by, though I have been less than diligent in verifying this possibility!

Burnbanks village, constructed in 1929 to house men working on the reservoir, is screened by trees and shrubs, now fully matured, though many of the original houses are either derelict or demolished.

Walkers who have followed the route over High Raise will rejoin the main line here.

In its final stages, the path to Burnbanks becomes a broad track, dropping to a stile by a gate. Descend through trees to a road leading to the cottages of this sheltered community.

As the road into Burnbanks is reached turn left for about forty or fifty metres to a gap in a wall on the right. A signpost reads: 'Coast to Coast Walk. Recommended route via Naddle Bridge, Thornthwaite Force and Park Bridge. By permission' and a delightful route it is, too.

Through the gap the way enters a charming woodland glade, echoing loudly in spring and summer to the

Burnbanks woodland

Old and New Naddle Bridges

song of wood, willow and garden warblers, a brief and cathartic gateway, cleansing body and mind of Lakeland splendour in preparation for a communion of a quite different order. Haweswater Beck gurgles peacefully, its water lapping moss- and ivy-covered rocks and boulders until, in no time at all, Naddle Bridge, is reached.

Cross the road to a stile giving onto a unique and fascinating configuration of bridges. Naddle Bridge itself is double-arched, while beside it, long usurped of its original function, stands a narrow grass-covered packhorse bridge. Within a few strides a small feeder stream, Naddle Beck, is crossed by a small wooden bridge.

Now go half left to amble along beside Haweswater Beck on a green path to a stile crossing a drystone wall. Once across the stile a few paces left brings Thornthwaite Force into view, a modestly proportioned cascade after which the beck assumes a broad and easy course, its banks enlivened in spring by the bright yellow of lesser celandine and marsh marigolds.

Heading downstream Park Bridge is soon encountered (pass on by), and after a short wander away from the stream a wider track forms, rising slightly to cross a side stream to a gate and step-stile. Turn right along a fenceline, climbing easily to High Park barn. Briefly there is a fine retrospective view of the fells surrounding

Mardale and the lower ground northwards of the Lowther valley.

Shortly after the barn bear half-left across pastureland to a prominent gate and stile, about 200m/yds away. Now cross two more fields to reach Rawhead Farm, where a stile gives on to the farm access, keeping right of the buildings to a minor metalled roadway.

Cross the road and traverse a short damp stretch before dropping to a road again near Rosgill Bridge.

Do not cross Rosgill Bridge but turn right through a gate on to a broad farm track with the river off to the left (signposted: 'Coast to Coast'). Stay along the track to a gate (stone step-stile nearby), through a gate and immediately left (do not climb the farm track) on a path beside the wall to a stile (slate signpost: 'Footpath to Shap Abbey'). The path continues until the wall ends and gives way to hawthorns (Goodcroft Farm up to the right), and then follows a fenceline to an area of small crags known as Fairy Crag. A few more minutes brings the way to a delectable corner where Parish Crag Bridge, double gated, spans Swindale Beck, a tributary of the Lowther.

Climb steeply above the bridge and cross the ensuing field, heading directly for an assortment of barns on the skyline. By stiles pass through the enclosure to reach a minor road at a corner.

Head up the road until the accompanying left hand wall breaks away, and here go left (signposted: 'Shap'). Bear obliquely right heading for a gate and stile, close by an electricity pylon. Cross the stile and an ancient dike that quickly follows to take a green path along a right-hand wall. As the wall bends right (waymark) follow it and then pull half-left across a field, climbing a small hillock. On the brow of the hillock Shap Abbey appears ahead and to the right, not immediately obvious in its surround of trees. Drop to a stile near a wall junction, and cross a final field before rejoining the Lowther.

Abbey Bridge leads into a small car park and on to the onward route, up the road, climbing away. The abbey, however, deserves a few moments, and is reached by going right (just before the bridge) along a broad track.

Rosgill Bridge spans the River Lowther which flows from Wet Sleddale to meet the Eamont near Penrith, and between here and Shap Abbey the way is never far from its company or influence.

SHAP ABBEY

The abbey at Shap was one of the many monastic houses established in England during the twelfth century. It belonged to an Order founded by the German Saint Norbert, and owes its foundation to a baron named Thomas son of Gospatric who held lands in Westmorland of William of Lancaster, the feudal lord of Kendale and Wyresdale. Towards the end of his life, Thomas son of Gospatric made arrangements for the establishment of an abbey on his own estates at Preston in Kendale, but before his death in 1201 he changed his mind and instead granted the canons a site twenty miles further north on the banks of the Lowther. He gave them leave to quarry stone and to fell timber on his land. The place where the abbey was founded was then known as 'Hepp', meaning 'a heap' and referring to the megalithic stone circle today known as Shap Stones. Less than a hundred years later the name changed from 'Hepp' to 'Hiap', and then to 'Shap'.

The new abbey was dedicated to St Mary Magdalene and sometimes referred to as 'St Mary Magdalene in the Valley'. Very little is known about the

Shap Abbey

history of the abbey; the Order was of Premonstratensian monks, and intended for those who wished to combine the life of prayer and discipline of a monk with parish work as priests serving local communities. Such men were known as 'White Canons' from the colour of the habits they wore. The history of such monastic Orders in England closes during the reign of Henry VIII, with the end for Shap coming on 14th January 1540, when the last abbot surrendered the abbey's possessions to the representatives of the Crown. For his co-operation, perhaps, he was compensated with what was then the comfortable pension of £40 per year, his canons receiving smaller sums sufficient at any rate for their subsistence.

The abbey lands were sold by the Tudor government to Sir Thomas Wharton, the governor of Carlisle, but in 1729, after the forfeiture of the Jacobite Duke of Wharton, they were purchased by Richard Lowther, of Mauld's Meaburn Hall. In 1948 the Lowther Estates Limited, as representatives of his descendant, Lancelot Edward Lowther, 6th Earl of Lonsdale, placed the abbey ruins in the guardianship of the Ministry of Works (now the Department of the Environment) for preservation as an Ancient Monument. Access is now permitted by the new custodians, English Heritage.

Walkers having diverted the short distance to visit Shap Abbey need now only leave the Abbey grounds and turn immediately right on an access road climbing (rather steeply, at this late stage in the day) to join the road to Shap only a short distance from the village. The main line of the way now follows the road into Shap, though from the corner at 555154 a path may be followed to meet Keld Lane. Turn left here for a short distance to the next corner, then right into a field, soon turning left through more fields to enter the village not far from the Market Hall.

Along the final stretch into Shap not-too-weary walkers may notice the change of bedrock from the granite of the Lakeland fells to the limestone that will now accompany the way. Not all the stones and boulders are limestone, however, for nearby, in the fields, are a number of huge boulders of granite. These are the Shap Stones (or Karl Lofts), thought by early historians to be relics of a mono-lithic monument: they are evidence of a double mile-long avenue of single boulders (megaliths) extending northwest from a stone circle just west of Hardendale Quarry at the southern end of the village.

The on-going route for the main line of the walk from Shap continues on page 77.

Variants: The following two variants cover the ground between The Knott and Burnbanks, and Kidsty Pike to Shap via Wet Sleddale.

HIGH RAISE RIDGE VARIANT

The Knott (Rampsgill Head) to Burnbanks via the High Raise ridge

Distance: (Patterdale to Shap)
24 kilometres (15 miles)
Ascent: 895 metres (2935 feet)

From the wall corner beneath The Knott continue along the path for the Straits of Riggindale, but soon climb left (east) up an easy slope leading to the top of Rampsgill Head. Follow the rim of the summit round, descending to a shallow col before the climb to the top of High Raise.

High Raise is the second highest summit of the High Street range, and northwards from it the ancient Roman road continues less evidently than to the south. The going along the line of the ridge is uncomplicated, though a little wet in places, passing first over the minor bumps of Raven Howe and Red Crag until Keasgill Head is reached (454160). From here a path (not a right-of-way) swings east around High Kop to join a right-of-way descending to Low Kop and Fordingdale Bottom. There is a right-of-way running southeast from just north of

Wether Hill, and walkers continuing as far as Loadpot Hill should use this on the return. (This short extension from Keasgill Head adds 3.5 kilometres (2.2 miles) to the day, with minimal additional ascent.)

Once Fordingdale Bottom is reached, cross Measand Beck by a footbridge and follow a line southeast to inspect The Forces before meeting the main line above the waters of the reservoir.

Walkers following this variant should now return to page 69 for the on-going route from Burnbanks.

Walkers following this variant should now return to page 69 for the on-going route from Burnbanks.

Suffering somewhat from an unappetising name, and of which it was once said 'if rain is stirring, the air scoops it surprisingly into the hollow of that dale', Sleddale, wet or dry, is a variant that will appeal to walkers seeking a little moorland escapism.

WET SLEDDALE VARIANT

Kidsty Pike to Shap via Wet Sleddale

Distance: (Patterdale to Shap):
26.5 kilometres (16.5 miles)
Ascent: 1235 metres (4050 feet)

This variant is a little more arduous than the main line, and takes a more southerly route to Shap crossing Gatescarth Pass to reach the head of Longsleddale before looping northeast to Mosedale and, finally, into Wet Sleddale. You are unlikely to be disturbed by other walkers along this stretch, the beauty of which lies in its wild loneliness where the call of the golden plover gives voice to the breeze.

From Kidsty Pike descend the long ridge to Bowderthwaite Bridge and cross the intervening ground to the foot of Rough Crag where a path rises easily to traverse The Rigg before heading for Mardale Head.

Near the car park at Mardale Head take a footpath (signposted: 'Longsleddale') and ascend southeast to the top of the pass, not an unduly difficult undertaking. Cross the pass and drop into the head of Longsleddale, a long and narrow valley through which flows the River Sprint. The pity is that the route cannot make more of Longsleddale, but Mosedale and its neighbour await.

From Brownhowe Bottom (478084) ascend easily

The Buttermarket, Keld

northeast to gain the head of Mosedale, following a path into Mosedale until, near the confluence of Mosedale Beck and Little Mosedale Beck, it is possible to cross the streams by a bridge and climb slightly over the broad expanse of Swindale Common into Wet Sleddale. The path through Wet Sleddale comes and goes, while the final section, from near the dam to Keld, though obvious enough and following a right-of-way, is virtually pathless.

The route enters Keld by a bridge where a metalled road is met. Follow the road out of Keld and shortly leave it to pursue a footpath across fields to Shap.

The on-going route description for the main line of the walk from Shap continues on page the next page.

2. LIMESTONE COUNTRY

Since 1970, when the M6 motorway was opened, Shap has been spared the aggravation of traffic that used to shake its very foundations. Not everyone applauded the single stroke of highway engineering genius that overnight brought peace and quiet to this straggling village high on the moorland fringe of the Lake District, for as tranquillity set in many jobs and livelihoods were lost. Once prosperous shops, hotels, cafés, garages and other sundry services faced an immediate decline in trade as everyone now by-passed the village, renowned for its snow-blocked winter roads that often ensnared a hopeful traveller.

Shops, cafés, hotels and boarding houses still remain, however, to resupply Coast to Coast walkers, but the economy of the village now largely rests on the prosperity of the nearby granite works and quarries, which add nothing to the otherwise wild beauty of the place.

Many of the houses date from the eighteenth century, grey and not a little forbidding, while its market hall with curious windows and round-headed arches dates from a few years after the village was granted a market charter in 1687. Quiet now, by comparison, but an important staging post for walkers travelling east or west.

Shap to Kirkby Stephen

Distance: 31.7 kilometres (19.8 miles)
Ascent: 535 metres (1755 feet)

As Shap is reached and passed, so the scenery becomes noticeably different, now entering the realms of limestone country, a welcome change after the ruggedness of the Lake District. Magnificent, refreshing scenery awaits, traversed without difficulty, but with few opportunities to break the otherwise lengthy trek to Kirkby

Stephen. The only village encountered is Orton, while walkers not constrained by time may consider dropping from the limestone pasturelands to Newbiggin-on-Lune an acceptable variant. Bents Farm, on the lower slopes of Crosby Garrett Fell, also offers the possibility of an overnight halt to shorten the day.

Walkers with a keen interest in pre-history will know that the ancient peoples of Britain found in this corner of Westmorland (as it used to be) much to their liking, and there are along and not far from this stretch of the walk many sites of archaeological and historical signifi-cance. This region, too, is abundant in wild life, and two large tracts of countryside are important breeding sites for birds across which there are precious few useful rights-of-way.

Taken in concert these special characteristics have necessitated careful route planning between Shap and Kirkby Stephen. This has only been possible with the help and advice of access officers working for the East Cumbria Countryside Project, and English Nature. There is still scope for improvement, and steps are being taken to achieve this: hopefully a route to the south of Sunbiggin Tarn, following an ancient track, will result before too long. If it does, some changes to waymarking may be encountered as a result. Walkers should not, as a rule, encounter access difficulties, but must remember that this is a remarkable and sensitive area from many *points of view, where routes are largely permissive. Where they are waymarked, please do adhere to the line, and, as ever, proceed with the utmost respect for the countryside and the people who earn their living from it.*

Leave the A6 on a signposted metalled roadway (Moss Grove) opposite the King's Arms Hotel at the southern end of the village. In a short while, follow the road to the right (signposted) and come to a broad farm access track. This quickly crosses the main north–south railway line, and continues parallel with the line for a short distance before heading east along an enclosed track with meadows on either side.

Just after a barn fork right on a green path, soon emerging, at a stile, into a field with a motorway footbridge prominent ahead. Cross the ensuing fields to reach the bridge.

While the view ahead, principally of the Shap granite works, is less than imposing, the retrospective view sweeps majestically from the distant Loadpot Hill, by way of High

continued on page 80

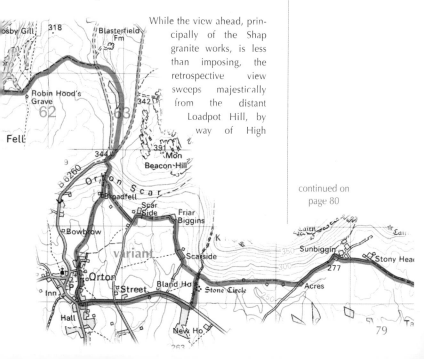

79

Raise, Kidsty Pike and High Street to the long grassy ridge of Kentmere Pike. Soon these glimpses of Lakeland will be fewer and then no more, replaced instead by fine, swelling domes to the south of the Howgills, as ahead the Pennine summits of Nine Standards Rigg, Mallerstang Edge and Wild Boar Fell start to capture our attention.

Cross the motorway bridge and continue right, parallel with the motorway for a short distance on a narrow path. At a corner of a walled pasture, and near a collapsed drystone wall, the path slants upwards and left through boulders and hawthorn to cross two temporary fences delineating underground pipeline works; the fences may well disappear in due course. A gate in the

En route for Kirkby Stephen

corner of a wall gives on to an open meadow near the isolated farm building, The Nab.

Beyond, and to the left, rises Hardendale Nab, a minor limestone summit much less now in stature than of old as huge chunks of it are removed from the, as yet unseen, Hardendale Quarry, though the quarry access road is plainly evident.

Not far away lies the hamlet of **Hardendale** itself, birthplace of **John Mill**, the Greek scholar who gave most of his life to transcribing the New Testament from manuscripts and died in 1707, two weeks after finishing a work that had taken him thirty years to complete. Here, too, is a farm where Bonnie Prince Charles and his officers stayed on the night of December 17, 1745, complaining about the high cost of food and the use of a room – not much changes!

Cross the minor road serving The Nab, and continue, aiming half-right on a green path to meet a wall. Ascend left a little, following the wall around to a gate, beside which there are notices warning of blasting in the quarry. Beyond the gate the path skirts along a limestone ledge before dropping to negotiate another stile leading to the quarry access road. Steps lead down to the road and up to the other side to a broad limestone plateau, soon rejoining another access road, though not one frequented by the huge lorries that travel the quarry access.

81

Oddendale Stone Circle

Oddendale is very much a shy and secluded place, a world apart from external haste and harassment. It lies at the heart of a vast area renowned for its wealth of prehistoric communities, no less than eleven early British settlements being found within a short compass. Oddendale Stone Circle, a double ring of stones, lies only a short distance from the Roman road, and is worth a short diversion.

The road now heads away for the hidden hamlet of Oddendale, but as it is approached, bear right, and shortly leave the road leading into Oddendale for a broad, gently rising track.

The track continues climbing easily as far as Potrigg, in reality no more than a barn on the edge of a walled enclosure, and surrounded by trees.

From the southern end of this enclosure the route continues as a permissive path only, along which the onward line (waymarked) starts by aiming left slightly for a group of conifers in a hollow, then bearing left to the remains of a sheep enclosure (marked on the map as a 'bield'), and keeps on to the corner of the conifer plantation, on a green path.

Ahead, now, a cairn can be seen on the edge of a limestone rise, and beyond it a signpost and another cairn mark the site of an ancient tumulus.

Before reaching the tumulus the walk crosses the line of Roman road linking forts at Low Barrow Bridge in Lonsdale, and Brougham.

Much of this area is popular with breeding birds, and the way across it is waymarked with the consent of the landowner: a good thing, too, for there is a grand feeling of openness here. Freed from the constraining summits and vales of Lakeland granite, the wind clears the mind (and sinuses), the sounds of moorland replace the subtly different music of the high fells, and the scenery rolls on forever to distant Cross Fell, the highest summit of the Pennines, and its acolytes, Little and Great Dun Fell, bringing an invigorating sense of freedom and self-satisfaction. Nearer to hand lies the serene loveliness of the Vale of Lyvennet, the onward route now substantially forming a ring around its headwaters.

The immediate onward route from the tumulus is not obvious, though a grassy trod shows the way through tussock grass to a limestone pavement beyond which a better path swings round to a large granite erratic at the top of a short descent to cross the infant Lyvennet Beck.

There are numerous 'alien' granite boulders, like those above Lyvennet Beck, dotted about the limestone country of the north. Brought to their final resting place at the whim of long-retreated glaciers, the larger ones, many with names, often serve the walker as useful guides, while more than a few have in the past been used to delineate parish boundaries.

Across the gathering grounds of Lyvennet Beck the route takes to a long enclosure wall as a guide, numerous tracks being formed by sheep, with a more prominent

Erratic boulder near the source of Lyvennet Beck

83

Crosby Ravensworth Fell is designated as a Site of Special Scientific Interest, an important area for nature conservation, and home to a range of moorland birds, some of which have declined significantly in recent years. Most notable of these are the golden plover, red grouse, redshank and curlew. These birds are characteristic of wild, isolated places, and are sensitive to disturbance, especially in the breeding season when they may desert the nest. Where the track across these moors is waymarked, you can help ease the difficulties for wildlife by following the waymarks closely, and keeping dogs with you under close control.

track, pressed from the land by walkers, leading to a wall corner.

Not far away, along the course of upper Lyvennet Beck, stands a monument at **Black Dub**, claimed to mark the source of the Livennet (sic). Erected in 1843 it more significantly commemorates the passage of King Charles II who, in 1651, here 'regaled his army and drank of the water on his march from Scotland.' Unfortunately, there is no legitimate route to the monument from the direction of travel, and erosional problems have been caused by walkers wandering indiscriminately over a wide area here.

Worthy of note is the fact, no longer in any way apparent on the ground, that the walk has here crossed the line of the first road from London to Scotland before the shelter, easier gradients, and more hospitable nature of the terrain through the Shap fells found favour.

From the wall corner head east, descending through low heather scrub to a shallow gorge, followed a short while later by a dried up stream bed.

The stream bed twists southwards and conceals, only a short distance away, a large pile of stones with the fanciful name '**Robin Hood's Grave**'. Now, the great Forest of Sherwood did extend much further north than

Robin Hood's grave

its present day residue; his trusty lieutenant, Little John, is said to lie buried in a churchyard in Hathersage in the Peak; Maid Marion, I have heard tell, originally came from Wakefield, and history undoubtedly does record that dear Robin travelled around quite a bit. But if the legendary hero's dying wish that he should be buried at the spot where his final arrow came to rest is to be believed, it would call for monumental quantities of credulity to believe he had the strength to flight it this far! His generally accepted resting place, if he existed at all, is at Kirklees, near Leeds.

Climbing easily, the route moves slowly away from the wall which has accompanied the way from Lyvennet Beck, and crosses a stretch of 'No-Man's Land' to head towards the minor road serving Crosby Ravensworth, reaching it directly opposite the Blasterfield Quarry, the only blemish on an otherwise perfect moorland landscape.

Follow the road, right, to the corner of a drystone wall enclosure, and then either continue on the road to its meeting with the road from Appleby, on the edge of Orton Scar, or leave the road again, once more on a permissive path (at least until the Orton road is rejoined), swinging round on a green path to the same point; the latter is simply easier underfoot.

Press on for 100m/yds to cross a cattle grid, and immediately descend, left, on a green cart track to a gate in a wall corner (Public Bridleway sign: 'Orton').

After the refreshing moorland traverse from Shap, arrival at the edge of Orton Scar is a most satisfying moment; the domed heights of the Howgills serve as a backdrop to the broad patchwork expanse of the Lune valley and the rising Pennines blue along the distant horizon. Even on a bleak day, the prospect of the onward journey to Kirkby Stephen is uplifting. The route, which here leaves it to you to decide whether to visit Orton, follows an interesting trek across numerous fields and access roads that eventually run out into open moorland. An alternative, a long, looping roadwalk passing north of, and way beyond, Sunbiggin Tarn, though speedy (and still available should you need it) is innately boring: it runs, too, along a road, albeit with good wide verges as a rule, that is nevertheless subject to the national speed limit of 60mph.

Walkers who are intentionally pottering their way coast to coast will find Orton one of the most charming of Westmorland villages, a most endearing and attractive overnight halt, though it arrives rather too soon for the speed merchants of long distance walking.

ORTON

Many of Orton's cottages date from the seventeenth and eighteenth century: Petty Hall, that once belonged to the Birkbeck family, bears the date 1604 on a panel over the doorway. Not far away stands Orton Hall, built in 1662, and for many years the home of the Burn family, one of whom acquired fame for his legal writings.

Surrounded by trees and built around a village green between two streams, Orton has a reputation for longevity, a considerable number of inhabitants having reached 100 years; it is as if the village goes so quietly about its business in so beautiful a setting that its inhabitants are reluctant to depart for the life hereafter, preferring, for the moment, the comforts of Orton's embrace.

Probably the most famous of Orton's inhabitants, however, was **George Whitehead**, one of the founders of the Society of Friends. Born here in 1636, he fell under the charismatic spell of George Fox, and, to the distress of his family, turned Quaker while still a youth. This was a most perilous time for Quakers, and while it is understandable that many folk in isolated communities like Orton should take to the faith, they were universally hated by Anglicans, Presbyterians, and Baptists alike, and it was commonplace to find people baiting them and beating them with sticks. Somehow, Whitehead survived this persecution and embarked on a personal crusade of a most remarkable order. Preaching widely, as George Fox had done, he argued at length with preachers and professors alike, visited imprisoned Quakers both willingly and then as a prisoner himself: he was placed in stocks, and whipped. Undaunted he held services on windswept hillsides, petitioned the House of Commons for justice for Quakers, and spent increasing periods of his life in prison.

Yet nothing, it seemed, could deter him from his

mission. In his quiet way he persuaded King Charles to free every captive Quaker, only to see them later thrown back into prison and robbed of their estates. From James II he secured immunity from persecution, but it was not until after the Revolution that Parliament passed an Act recognising Quakers as citizens.

If George Fox was the creator of the Society of Friends, George Whitehead, it has been said, 'was the law-giver, the Moses of his creed.' Unabashed, he stood before seven sovereigns, obtaining concessions that later found their way into the Quaker Magna Carta of 1696. He died in 1723, aged 86.

Walkers not wishing to visit Orton should see below for a more direct continuation.

Beyond the gate follow the curving green path downwards (disused lime kiln on the left) towards woodland, and there, through a gate, keep ahead, following the right-hand field boundary and aiming to the right of Broadfell Farm buildings, and thereafter keeping generally ahead on a delightful bridleway, through gates, to enter the village by a quiet back road.

Leave Orton on the road past the inn, heading left at the southern end of the village to follow the road to Raisebeck (B6261). After about 1.5 kilometres (1 mile) the unsurfaced track of Knotts Lane shoots off to the left. Follow this until, shortly after two trees and the remains of a barn on the right, you reach a double gate and stile (400m/yds).

> Before reaching the gates note, over the wall on the right, the **Gamelands Stone Circle**, a circle of considerable size with many of its original forty or so stones remaining.

This same point may be reached by a more direct route, given here, from the edge of Orton Scar, for walkers who are not visiting Orton.

Descend from near Orton Scar, past the woodland, and through the gate north of Broadfell Farm. Now go left, following a wall, to meet the farm access.

Follow the farm access out to Street Lane, a minor road serving a handful of isolated farms. Go left up the lane to Scar Side Farm, then east along a gated section to Friar Biggins Farm, and, shortly, Scarside Farm. Here, just after the farm buildings, a gate on the left gives access to a field. Climb slightly left to a newish fence-line, and stay with this closely along an uncultivated field margin until a wall is encountered. Follow the wall round to a gate and stile, giving on to Knott Lane, a long-established bridleway leading north in to Orton Scar.

Stride across Knott Lane to a couple of gates and another stile giving access to a field; it is here that the two routes reunite.

Cross the stile at the gates and follow the right boundary wall away on an indistinct bridleway, keeping the wall on the right until the path goes through a narrow gate at a wall corner (643083), so passing to the other side of the wall.

Continue eastwards on an improving path, crossing a number of north–south walls and enclosures, and a few larger pastures, eventually to reach another minor metalled lane at Acres Farm. Go left along the lane, to Sunbiggin Farm, and there head east for Stony Head Farm, where the lane surrenders to a broad green trail enclosed between walls (signposted: 'Bridleway to Sunbiggin Tarn'), leading to a meeting of rights-of-way at 672084, at a tall fingerpost.

The short stretch of road between Acres Farm and the Sunbiggin hamlet is narrow and often used by farm vehicles and for herding sheep and cattle. Take care as you pass along not to cause any inconvenience, or to put yourself at risk of a confrontation of a bovine or other nature.

Continue ahead from the fingerpost on a clear path to a gap stile (with metal bars) in a wall (waymark). Beyond the wall the path disappears, but heads roughly northeast, reaching the Asby road about 500m/yds (southwest of its junction with the Newbiggin road, to which the route now continues. There is no right-of-way across the apex of this road junction, from where a delightful and undulating road walk ensues, past a group of houses at Mazon Wath, and as far as a conspicuous turning on the left about 300m/yds south of a cattle grid, towards the raised mound of a reservoir.

Walkers bound for Newbiggin-on-Lune instead of turning left at the reservoir should continue ahead down the road to the village; a little over one kilometre (half a mile) distant. The onward route the next day may be rejoined either by returning up the Asby road, or by taking the minor road, leaving the main road just east of the village, leading to Friar's Farm, from where a good track leads to Smardale Bridge, there rejoining the main route.

There is, too, a suggestion that an alternative way may be found, running south of Sunbiggin Tarn. It is pleasant enough, but rests on an ancient track across Ravenstonedale Moor, omitted from the Definitive Rights-of-Way Plan, being granted footpath status. Even then it will involve backtracking, in quite the wrong direction, to make it accessible.

Continue past the reservoir, then keep east along the north side of a wall towards Ewe Fell Mire, normally nothing like as desperate as its name suggests. Eventually the path broadens out into a multiplicity of ways, cultivated as much by sheep as people, and leads to a gate not far from a barn. Press on past the barn keeping a wall on the right and ignoring any paths branching off to the left.

> The easy crossing above the Crosby Garrett Fell intake is delightful strolling, with time aplenty to take in the view. Away to the right the Howgills, that have kept company with the walk since Orton Scar, are starting now to recede, replaced by the great swell of Wild Boar Fell, the Vale of Eden, Mallerstang Edge, Hugh Seat and Nine Standards Rigg. From the vicinity of Bents Farm an ambitious eye might just pick out the cairns on Nine Standards Rigg.

Continue following the intake wall, and, near a cluster of sheepfolds, press on through a gate in an intermediate wall. Keep along the ensuing wall until, at a prominent waymark, you can cross it by a stile.

During much of the walk to reach the Asby road there are fine views of Sunbiggin Tarn to the south. The tarn, though undoubtedly a welcome oasis in these great uplands, is another sensitive area. The raucous clamour of hundreds of breeding gulls will pinpoint its whereabouts sooner by sound than by sight, and therein lies the principal reason for giving the tarn area a wide berth. The area around the tarn, boasting no rights-of-way, is another Site of Special Scientific Importance.

Smardale Bridge is an ideal spot for a short rest before the final lap to Kirkby Stephen. The stream here is Scandal Beck, and its banks in spring play host to a wide variety of wild flowers among which are dog roses, herb robert, and monkeyflower, while the stream itself is often covered with great rafts of white-flowered river water-crowfoot.

Smardale Bridge

Ignore the clear trod going ahead, but go immediately left along a wall, keeping above the settlement, and ultimately descending through geologically fascinating limestone outcrops and steps, to reach a dilapidated building that once served the disused railway line, part of the former Tebay–Darlington line. Near the building follow a green path to the right, to reach a gated bridge crossing the line, and turn right (ignoring the low stile across a fence on the right), to continue along the fence, following a curving path descending to Smardale Bridge. It is especially important to follow the waymarking closely across this section since the way has encroached on the Severals settlement, a prehistoric British village.

The significance of the **Severals settlement** cannot be underestimated; it is a most remarkable place. Alas, for walkers very little is plainly visible at ground level.

The site is listed as one of key importance to our understanding of living conditions thousands of years ago. The remains we see today are limited, and fully understood only by those knowledgeable in matters archaeological. Most of the settlement lies to the south of the wall crossed earlier, though there are traces of two

other settlements north of the wall, overlooking the wooded gate of Scandal Beck. Mark your passage with a moment's pause to let your mind run free, back into time…

Running north from Smardale Bridge, the valley of *Smardale* is very attractive, and little known outside the immediate locality. The former railway has left a few scars and disused buildings, but its great viaduct is a wonder to behold. The flanks of the old railway line are renowned for a wide variety of wild flowers, including many not widely seen, and, if your interest lies here, a short detour, using the low stile just after the railway bridge mentioned earlier, will bring ample reward.

At a number of sites near Smardale Bridge the maps mention **'Pillow Mounds'** closer inspection reveals that these are not natural formations, and are known locally as **'Giants' Graves'**, though their true origin is uncertain. Various notions have been advanced about them, including the suggestion (quite probable) that they were rabbit warrens constructed by the monks who farmed this area.

Cross Smardale Bridge, beyond which the onward path awaits, climbing easily by a drystone wall to a stile across a low fence. Rising easily, never far from the wall, the path arrives at a gate and ladder-stile before setting off, this time in parallel with a long and unusually thin enclosure to cross the northern flanks of Smardale Fell before descending to a gate and stile at a minor road, leading left to Waitby.

On the springy-turfed descent to the minor road there are fine views ahead of the high moorland Pennines of tomorrow, sweeping round from the now prominent Nine Standards to the haven of the Vale of Eden, framed between Mallerstang Edge and Wild Boar Fell. Closer to foot, the path, largely a spaghetti-like tangle of rutted tracks, crosses Limekiln Hill, deriving its name from the proximity of two kilns, just off the path, but one at least worthy of a short detour.

Turn right on reaching the road to a junction 150m/yds away, and then left, slightly downhill, for another 150m/yds, leaving the road by a through stile (sign-posted: 'Coast to Coast: Public Footpath to Kirkby Stephen').

Diagonally cross the meadow that follows on a green path aiming for a solitary tree near a wall corner. Swing round, left, at the tree, pass a barn and continue to the railway underpass ahead.

> The railway is the **Settle–Carlisle line**, a route much-loved by railway enthusiasts, and a stark reminder of the Midland Railway's determination to construct its own route to Scotland; it was built at enormous cost both in terms of finance and of human life. During the 1980s, affected by the ravages of time and the sheer inhos-pitability of the climate, the future of the railway was called into question as the old spectre of financial viability once more reared its ugly head. A vigorous campaign to keep the line open was finally vindicated in April 1989, when the Government announced that the line was to remain open. Its numerous viaducts and tunnels, notably further south, near Ribbleshead, and the regular steam locomotive excursions organised by enthusiasts for enthusiasts, will long remain as a testa-ment to Victorian endeavour and achievement.

Go through the underpass and across the next field to a stile (waymark), continuing on a grassy path through a slight depression.

> Just after the underpass there is yet more evidence of early settlements, among a scattering of hawthorns, on the right.

More waymarks guide the path to a gate and narrow lane leading between the obsolete abutments of a dismantled railway to turn right into a farmyard at Green Riggs. A waymark affixed to a kennel shows the way out onto the farm access, leading to a back lane into Kirkby Stephen.

Just after leaving Green Riggs Farm the remains of **Croglam Castle**, no more than a rampart and a ditch, stand in the field on the right, accessible, if you have the energy and the inclination, by a stile. The site is thought to have been one of many hill forts constructed by the Brigantes before the coming of the Romans.

The back lane, improving, marginally, as Kirkby Stephen is approached, may be followed all the way into town, keeping very much away from the rather busier main street (A685), thought the latter may be joined at any one of a number of points. In the end, an alleyway leads right, to the Black Bull Inn (how convenient!), while a short way further, a counterpart favours the Pennine Hotel, directly opposite the Market Place, from where the onward route departs.

Walkers bound for the youth hostel should either join the A685 by one of the earlier opportunities, or turn right on reaching the main street near the Market Place.

Many walkers will have traversed this section from Shap in one day, and will no doubt welcome the chance to put their feet up, and maybe a few pints down! Others may have wandered across rather more leisurely, stopping, perhaps at Orton. But few will have done either without acquiring a sense of ancient occasion, a passage through time, extending two, three, maybe four thousand years into the dawn of man's time in northern Britain. Opportunities to experience so much in so, relatively, short a distance are few; only a soulless, blinkered person could pass by without so much as a thought for our prehistory, and, thankfully, very few of those have the spirit or imagination it takes to become walkers.

And if this ancient fantasy land has aroused something within you, make sure it is well secured in your memory before advancing into the traffic-busy streets of Kirkby Stephen. The sudden return to the late twentieth-century may come as something of a culture shock!

3. INTO THE DALES

KIRKBY STEPHEN

An old market town, with a charter since 1351, Kirkby Stephen gives the impression of a place that doesn't quite know what it wants to be: an overgrown village, tightly built up for a while, but lacking any real depth, gathering its shape 'and what importance it possesses as much from being on the road to somewhere else as from what it is in itself.' First impressions are that it is larger than it really is, but the River Eden, slipping quietly round the back of the town, rather sharply defines its eastern boundaries, while low hill pastures start to rise within 100 metres of the town's main road, to the west.

Though lying on the once-important route up the Eden valley to Carlisle, the town, down the centuries, has been overshadowed by its neighbour, Brough, whose massive castle dominated the strategic junction of the Carlisle route with the road by Stainmore from Scotch Corner, formerly the main road from London to Scotland.

Frank's Bridge, Kirkby Stephen

Alas, the coming of the railways signalled Brough's ultimate decline, and by 1860 it was little more than a village, the railway having effectively wiped out the coaching trade it used to enjoy. Bad news for Brough, but good news for Kirkby Stephen, for the railways passed close by, and until fairly recently the town could boast the luxury of two railway stations; now only the Settle–Carlisle line remains. As Kirkby Stephen expanded, its Luke Fair replaced Brough Hill Fair as a mecca for cattle and sheep sales, and even when the tangled network of railways met the economic cuts of the Beeching axe, Kirkby still survived on the strength of the expanding motor trade, proving a well-sited staging post for convoys of charabancs taking northeast workers on holiday and day trips to Blackpool illuminations. In those heady days of wealth, a café in Kirkby was a licence to print money, and the whole town, bent on victualling tired and emotional Geordies, stayed bright-eyed, bushy-tailed, and occasionally legless well into the early hours.

Coaches still stop there, spilling trippers into its gift shops, cafés, market and pubs, while the Coast to Coast Walk sees to it that a steady plod of hungry wayfarers finds its weary way into the town in search of hotels, bed and breakfasts, campsites, and the youth hostel.

Kirkby's church of St Stephen is worth a visit. Rather like a small cathedral, it still bears traces of Saxon and Norman handiwork. In the former county of Westmorland, St Stephen's was second in size only to the church at Kendal, and has a stately nave notable for its length and its magnificent thirteenth-century arcades. Dalemen have worshipped on the site since Saxon times, and, until the early part of the twentieth-century, heard curfew rung from the sixteenth-century tower each evening.

The old town was built for defence against border raiders, with narrow, high-walled passages and spacious squares into which cattle would be driven in times of danger; indeed, those narrow passages provide the lynch pin for at least one local legend. Two salmon poachers, it is claimed, escaped from the long arm of the law by fleeing in their Mini down the narrow confines of Stoneshot. The pursuing police, coming from Penrith, and lacking essential local knowledge, endeavoured to follow in their patrol car only to find themselves wedged between the walls, unable to go forward or back, or open the doors. Whether true or not, the very idea gives rise to a happy thought with which to set off for Swaledale.

Kirkby Stephen to Keld

Distance: 17.8 kilometres (11 miles)
Ascent: 515 metres (1690 feet)

Between Kirkby Stephen and Keld the walk crosses the watershed of Britain, but the conditions underfoot have seriously deteriorated on the popular ascent of Nine Standards Rigg, creating a difficult surface for walkers and considerable environmental damage. Moreover, part of the ascent, from Rollinson's quarry onwards, and, for that matter, the well-established path down from Nine Standards Rigg, across White Mossy Hill to Ravenseat, has not followed a right-of-way. To combat this latter problem, the Yorkshire Dales National Park and the landowner have together laid out an alternative route that should be acceptable to everyone. This cuts directly down into Whitsun Dale from just south of Nine Standards Rigg, and follows Whitsundale Beck to Ravenseat.

At certain times of year, when the conditions are

especially poor, deviations are in operation along this section.

Leave the Market Place (opposite the Pennine Hotel) by a short lane past public conveniences, and descending Stoneshot (of poachers fame!) to swing left and meet the River Eden at Frank's Bridge.

The River Eden finds its source high up on the slopes of Mallerstang, on Black Fell Moss, not far, in fact, from the birthplace of the Ure, and the Swale, the river that will shortly accompany the walk for a good part of the remainder of the journey. The Eden, rising in a wild and magnificent setting, soon settles down to a sedate meander through its lush and fertile vale, finally condescending to meet the Solway Firth near Carlisle.

To gaze on Eden's loveliness is to appreciate how apt is its name 'fetched from paradise and rightfully borne' (Wordsworth): to travel its length is quite another story, and one evocatively told by Neil Hanson, sometime landlord of the Tan Hill Inn, in his book Walking through Eden.

continued on page 98

Cross Frank's Bridge, where an ever-present assembly of ducks sets up a cacophony of appeals for food, and turn right courting the river for a short distance until it swings away, right, and there to follow

97

a path ahead, through gates, and by a quiet lane into Hartley.

The hamlet of **Hartley** is a delightful place on the road to nowhere: as Arthur Mee comments in The Lake Counties: 'A company of limes by a stream, silver birches, a little bridge, a few houses below the grandeur of the Pennines, this is Hartley, a quiet spot under a hill over 2000 feet high, with nine great stone cairns centuries old.'

The conventional route to Nine Standards summit has deteriorated drastically in recent years, and since most walkers reaching the summit are reluctant to omit a visit to the Nine Standards themselves (nor should they!), the inevitable erosion problem could be halved by a more direct route to the great cairns; this is what the ascent by way of Faraday Gill provides.

Go right, through Hartley for a while to a path on the left (signposted: 'Hikers and Walkers to Nine Standards and Whitby') descending to cross Hartley Beck by a clapper footbridge, and then on to the road climbing to the vicinity of Hartley Quarry. Continue with the fell road, climbing steadily towards Fell House Farm, a rather isolated outpost, where at last the gradient eases. The road runs on to its demise at a fork, where the way follows the left branch (signposted: 'Bridleway to Nine Standards Rigg' – though it only goes as far as the quarry) rising through a gate and on to Hartley Fell.

Continuing as a broad track the onward route is never in doubt, and soon joins company with a wall (on the right), near a disused barn. Keep ahead, shortly crossing Faraday Gill, and then climbing easily, always following the wall.

Faraday Gill, incidentally, commemorates the local family whose offspring, **Michael Faraday** (1791–1867), was the physical scientist who discovered electromagnetic induction and other important electrical and magnetic phenomena.

Near a bend in the wall a Land Rover track dips down to the left to cross the gill at a ford. Ignore this, continuing along the line of the wall to a point where a small cairn and a fingerpost mark a broad green track heading off the stony track, and leading first into a sunken pathway and then back towards Faraday Gill once more. As the gill is reached it becomes more deeply incised, and offers a moment's diversion in a series of miniature cascades. Shortly, the route arrives at a pile of stones named as 'Faraday House' on old maps, surmounted by two large cairns, with another cairn raised from more piles of stones, on the other side of the gill. This is the end of the track, and beyond lies rougher walking for a while, leading across the gill directly behind Faraday House. Ignore the more obvious path going slightly left to the gill, but pursue instead a more direct trod aiming for the Nine Standards, soon crossing the gill at a bend

Faraday Gill

On Nine Standards Rigg

in its course, and continuing as a broader (and wet) path easily to the summit ridge.

Arrival at the **Nine Standards** is a moment of some occasion: it lies on the watershed of Britain, that great north–south divide sending waters one way to the Irish Sea, and the other to the North Sea, though there are times and rainy days when you gain the distinct impression it sends them nowhere at all!

No one has yet come up with any historical fact about the origins or purpose of the Nine Standards. They stand on the former county boundary between Westmorland and the North Riding of Yorkshire, and, more than likely, their origin derives from that significance, though one fanciful notion suggests they were built to persuade marauding Scots that an English army was camped up there, which as Neil Hanson points out 'suggests a contempt for Scottish intelligence that even the English would find hard to maintain.'

On a clear and fine day there are few places that give a wider, more inspiring, panorama of the massive sprawling beauty of the wild moorlands of northern England than Nine Standards. It is the most far-reaching view seen on the crossing, extending from the mounds of Cross Fell, the Dun Fells and Mickle Fell in the north to the lofty escarpment of Wild Boar Fell across the upper Vale of Eden. It is truly a place apart; somewhere certainly to take a break: somewhere to cast your eyes back the way you have come, to the now hazy-blue Lakeland heights. From here we head into dales, Swaledale in particular, and though there is nothing to come that is higher than Nine Standards, it would be a mistake to think it was now all downhill. Yet you cannot help thinking about what lies ahead; somewhere, down that long valley sandwiched between the grouse moors of Rogan's Seat and the bogs of Great Shunner Fell, lies journey's end – a pleasing thought, and a sad one.

The highest point of Nine Standards Rigg occurs at the trig point, a short way to the south. Between the Nine Standards and the trig an orientation table has been erected by the Kirkby Stephen Fell Rescue Team.

Go south from the Nine Standards to the trig, and follow a broad path heading for White Mossy Hill. Shortly after crossing a peaty drainage channel that marks the county boundary leave the forward path and head left, following a line of marker posts (signposted: 'Alternative route to Ravenseat') across moorland terrain, and descend, keeping north of Craygill Sike, to that stream's eventual confluence with Whitsundale Beck.

Keeping on the west side of Whitsundale Beck, continue along its course to the fenced enclosures of Fawcett Intake, where a stile facilitates onward progress. The route throughout the dale tends to keep above the stream, preferring the flanks of adjoining moorland to the twists and turns of the dale bottom. On emerging from the confines of the dale, near some delightful shallow falls, the path approaches a cross-wall. Here swing right, continuing to follow the waymarked route, and keeping the wall on the left as it leads to a low shelter with a domed corrugated iron roof (a rough emergency shelter). Cross the nearby fence and descend to Ney Gill. Go left along the wall, passing a sheep dipping enclosure until, at a wall corner, the path is forced to cross Ney Gill, then climb easily alongside a wall (on the left), soon to swing round and down to meet a minor road at a cattle grid, by which the route enters the farming community of Ravenseat.

Whitsun Dale is a charming retreat, echoing to the call of curlew, buzzard and golden plover, where, on balmy days, the breeze sighs a soft accompaniment to a melody of light and shade, herons patrol the stream, and the miles that have gone and are to come seem like a distant world. Close by, the ever-growing beck fashions an indolent course, unhurried, reluctant yet to seek out its fate, not far hence. Sheepfolds proliferate, their sometime occupants dotted about the fellsides, but there is otherwise little to betray the hand of man in this secluded spot.

Cross the bridge at Ravenseat and immediately go right across a narrow sleeper bridge over a small stream to a gate. Pass through the gate and shortly turn right again through a gated stile setting the route along the eastern bank of Whitsundale Beck.

The onward route is never in doubt, pleasant walking now ensues, the beck never far distant and providing some attractive waterfalls to enhance an already appealing scene. Continue easily, negotiating a number of gates through walls, climbing half-left to a barn, and then by a slightly higher level to the quite surprising scenery of How Edge Scars and Oven Mouth, where, over countless years, the stream has done remarkable things to the landscape. If by chance you wander inadvertently off the route onto a conspicuous lower path, you are brought much closer to Oven Mouth, escaping from the folds of the stream by a steeply ascending path climbing left alongside a wall.

Above Oven Mouth, and after a gate in a fence, the path forks. Go right here to pass a dilapidated enclosure, Eddy Fold, until the farmstead of Smithy Holme is reached. A good path goes past the farm and soon drops to meet the Kirkby Stephen–Keld road at Low Bridge,

Ravenseat Bridge

from where Keld and its youth hostel are but a short distance away.

But you don't have to quit the high level route just yet. After a gate just before the final drop towards Low Bridge look for a path going left above a collapsed wall. This leads above a limestone escarpment, Cotterby Scar, to meet the road climbing (left) to Tan Hill at a hairpin bend. At the road turn right and descend to the valley road for the final moments to Keld. Unless going to the youth hostel (a short way ahead), go left at the first junction and descend to the village.

KELD

Until the Pennine Way found its way into this upper reach of the Swale, Keld was virtually unknown outside the dale. It is an ancient settlement of Scandinavian origin, its name, from the Norse, meaning 'a place by the river'.

The hamlet is attractively situated, the first village in Swaledale, surrounded by high moorlands, with the river bullying its way through the dale, crashing in a series of spectacular falls, or 'forces', out to the broader, greener pastures of Richmond and beyond. Catrake Force and Kisdon Force are the best of the cascades, though each limestone lip in the riverbed sets up a foaming flurry of activity at the surface as the peaty brown water flows on.

Once remote, it seems now that Keld has taken keenly to what benefits the Pennine Way, in particular, has brought in the way of travellers seeking a bed and nourishment; a youth hostel has been provided along the 'main' road, bed and breakfast signs adorn a few old and attractive buildings, and one of the farms offers a campsite, farmhouse accommodation and a range of refreshments. But even so, the opportunities for an overnight stay, however delightful a prospect, are limited, and prebooking a good idea. Fortunately, many of the proprietors in this distant corner of the Dales recognise the difficulties (and needs) of walkers, and a brief telephone call is often all that is needed to bring a

The infant River Swale at Keld

car whizzing from some remote farmstead to whisk you away to luxuries and friendliness that are typical of the region.

Not so long ago many of these 'isolated' communities largely managed their own affairs; Keld held its own sports day, Muker boasted a brass band, and all of them, not surprisingly, had their own characters: in Keld it was Dick Alderson, better known as Neddy Dick. Neddy's particular claim to fame, so it is said, was his ability to make music from stones. Apparently, while climbing near Kisdon Force one day, he dislodged a sliver of rock and heard a distinct musical ring as it fell against other rocks. Before long he found enough rocks to compose a 'limestone scale', on which he would accompany his own singing. His great ambition, alas unfulfilled, was to go on tour with his geological one-man band piled on a donkey cart! Does the world know what it missed, I wonder?

Keld, by the way, is roughly the half way point; and what lies ahead is every bit as good as what has been left behind (whichever way you are going).

Keld to Reeth

Distance: 17 kilometres (10.5 miles)
Ascent: 545 metres (1790 feet)

Between Keld and Reeth there is a choice of routes, one swings high on to the moorland where it affords a thorough inspection of the remains of the lead mining industry that once flourished in these parts. The other faithfully courts the River Swale. The former, a sad trek through the rubble and ruins of a hard but once-proud industry, is nevertheless a must for anyone with an interest in industrial archaeology or geology, while the latter will appeal to those who enjoy riverside rambles, a spectacular display of wild flowers, and the conviviality of rural pubs (of which there are quite a number). The only drawback with the low level option is the considerable quantity of what I call 'squeeze' stiles; the aptness of the description, to anyone of ample proportions, soon becomes obvious, and has caused me to suggest the name 'Fat Man's Agony' (not a sexist comment, by the way) for virtually the whole stretch, certainly between Muker and Reeth. Walkers with short legs and large packs may also experience some (not insurmountable) difficulty, though on balance the varying degrees of success and ingenuity of all walkers in negotiating these man-made obstacles are more likely to result in mirth and merriment than mayhem and mishap, and should deter no one from choosing this option.

The low level route is given below as a variant, and it is a great pity that the two routes cannot be combined. I mean, no one in their right mind, having scampered across the high level route, would think of taking a taxi back to Muker the next day to tackle the low level route just because it was outstandingly beautiful, would they? Or would they?

Though not intended to sway a decision away from the high level route, it should be borne in mind that much of it can be confusing in mist; miners' tracks and sledgates radiate in all directions, the litter of man's industry abounds, and however precise a worded description, the potential for error is not insignificant. In poor visibility, the Swale option, with its riverside paths and country lanes, is undoubtedly the wiser choice.

Leave Keld by a rough lane running southeast (sign-posted: 'Kisdon Force' and 'Muker'), and soon branch left, and down, to cross the Swale by a footbridge.

Friarfold
Moor

Friarfold
Rake

Mines
(dis)

Level Ho
(ruin)

Moor Ho

B E C K S   M O O R

Reeth High Moor

Barras End

·578

97   98

Mill
Bottom

Feetham Pastu

Nearby, the Swale is augmented
by the waters of East Gill, making its
head-on entrance in a series of miniature
cascades, a perfect overture to the rich harmonies that
flow from the Swale throughout its length.

continued on
page 108

This brief crossing of the Swale is something of a
meeting place, a passage in common with the Pennine
Way, which here swaggers in from Thwaite and Great
Shunner Fell only to depart moments later en route for
Tan Hill as if intolerant of impertinent young pretenders
to its regal position as Britain's premier long distance
path. Any Pennine Wayfarers encountered here should
be treated with a measure of sympathy; they are leaving
the beauties of upper Swaledale for the bleak moors of
Tan Hill. Coast to Coasters, meanwhile are heading for
paradise. The present footbridge over the Swale is on the
site of a packhorse bridge, destroyed by floods in 1899.

Above East Gill Force the onward route is signposted,
through a gate and climbing impressively above Kisdon
Gorge, and soon, at a fork, branching left to the ruins of
Crackpot Hall.

Crackpot Hall, commanding a superlative position above
the Swale, would once have been a most attractive farmhouse. Alas, subsidence, caused by the mining activities,
hastened its demise, an end that came in the 1950s, and
an event that must surely have saddened its occupants in
spite of the no doubt punishing existence that life among
these isolated farming communities entailed. The farmhouse was built by Lord Wharton for his keeper, who

Throughout much of the journey towards Reeth there is evidence in abundance of the mining activities that once took place here – ruined smelt mills, chimneys, flues, old shafts, levels, hushes, spoil heaps, wheel pits, watercourses, reservoirs, and dams. Though in the eyes of some they mar the landscape, they also form an essential ingredient of importance and interest to those who view the walk as a journey through time and history as well as a satisfying way of passing a couple of weeks.

managed the red deer that roamed the wooded hillsides of the seventeenth century. Tempting as it may seem so to think, the name of the farm is no comment on the mental state of its occupants, deriving instead from the 'pot' (i.e. pot hole or cave) of the crows.

Lead mining probably began in the Dales before the Romans came, but the first clear evidence comes from pigs of smelted lead bearing the names of Roman Emperors, discovered at Hurst Mines, just north of Reeth, and near Grassington in Wharfedale. The industry was also carried out by the Anglo-Saxons, by monks of the many monasteries and priories that dotted the pre-Henry VIII English landscape, and during Tudor times. But the activity reached its peak during the late eighteenth and early nineteenth centuries, and most of the physical remains that are encountered on the walk are relics of that time.

Just before reaching the ruins of Crackpot Hall, for example, the path crosses the line of Old Field Hush, a grooved scouring of the hillside caused by the artificial damming of water up above, which, when released, flushed surface debris and soil away to reveal much-prized minerals and ore, or at least the suggestion that a vein of ore might be present. The Old Field Hush was worked from 1738 to 1846, during a time of much squabbling between the Parkes brothers, owners of nearby Beldi Hill Mines, and Lord Pomfret, whose mines were in Swinner Gill.

Walkers electing to pursue the low level route through Swaledale should now refer to pages 113–117.

Continue on the track rising behind Crackpot Hall, and past buildings of a former smithy. The view down the valley towards Muker is here quite exhilarating as the path becomes narrow and rocky, turning under the crumbling sandstone outcrops of Buzzard Scar and into the awesome gorge of Swinner Gill.

> At the head of the gill, at the junction with Grain Gill, is a fine stone bridge, while across the bridge are the ruins of Swinnergill Mines, with dressing floors and the decaying hulk of the smelt mill. The mineral veins worked by the lead miners are especially numerous on the north side of Swaledale; the veins run approximately W–E and NW–SE, so that the four tributaries of the Swale, of which Swinner Gill is the first, cut across a complex of veins allowing them to be discovered and worked. Swinner Gill well illustrates this, and further evidence awaits in Gunnerside Gill, Hard Level Gill and Arkle Beck.
>
> In the gorge to the left of upper Swinner Gill lies Swinnergill Kirk, in reality a cave where, during times of religious persecution, those of the Catholic faith would meet and pray in secret. Quite why, having struggled so far into the wild heartland of these rolling hillsides, the necessity would still be felt to seek out the seclusion of a cave is unclear, but it invests an otherwise bleak and inhospitable spot with a dash of much needed colour. Botanists will also find a diversion into the gill of interest, for its damp atmosphere and wet rocks and ledges are home to a host of unusual flowers, ferns, mosses and liverworts.

Beyond the ruins of the smelt mill the path climbs stiffly for a while along the line of East Grain, the gradient easing just before the broad scar of a shooters' track is encountered. Now follow the track to the left, climbing easily to the highest point on the moor, just after a fence, and near a distinct branch to the left leading to the summit of lonely Rogan's seat.

Little more than a century ago the long ravine of **Gunnerside Gill** was a scene of intense mining activity. It is visited now only by walkers and those with an interest in industrial archaeology; for the latter it must be a wonderland, for, in spite of its present day quiet, little imagination is needed to call forth the sounds of men labouring hard and long hours, often with bare hands and primitive tools.→

The remains of Blakethwaite Mine, Gunnerside Gill

As the high point of this stretch is reached there is a glimpse, right, of *Moss Dam*, a relic of the mining days, almost concealed now by the ever-encroaching heather.

Continue ahead, descending gently as far as an enclosure on the left made of stones and corrugated iron sheets. A short way ahead the main track bends right to head for Gunnerside. Before reaching this point look for two smallish cairns on the left, leading to a larger one. Leave the main track at this point and follow a narrow path heading towards Gunnerside Gill. For a while the path skims along the rim of North Hush before moving away, northeast, to descend, steeply in places, to Blind Gill and the remains of the Blakethwaite Lead Mine.

Cross the stream by a slab bridge to reach the cloistered remains of a once fine building, thought to be a smelt mill.

Behind the smelt mill take a path steeply zigzagging up the hillside to meet a green, terraced pathway. Turn right along this, with fine views down towards Gunnerside, and continue in airy fashion as far as Friarfold Hush, and then towards Bunton Hush.

The scenery is confusing here, a mess of spoil, litter, gullies, hushes and collapsed walls, and though a

The ruins of Old Gang Lead Mine (High Level Route)

number of gullies all lead to the moors above, that beneath a conspicuous fractured cliff has rather more sense of purpose and rises easily to a low grassy ridge, on the right, where a line of cairns is encountered, heading safely round and up to the highest ground. Here, by a large cairn, a broad gravel track is met, and followed ahead, through continuing devastation, with barely a blade of grass in evidence, to the Old Gang Mines at the head of Old Gang Beck.

← That this mangled landscape is a mess is obvious; it would take a tolerant eye to find beauty here, yet it is a compelling place to visit, and, ironically, a perfect counterpoint to the surfeit of natural beauty that is Swaledale.

> In spite of the unremitting barrenness of the terrain, there is never any doubt about the onward route once the high moorland is reached, though there is precious little in the way of shelter for anyone caught out by a sudden change in the weather. The heath-clad moors are gone, replaced by the desolation that only man can achieve, but awesome in its bleakness.

Flincher Gill is crossed by a stone bridge, beyond which the track continues as roughly as ever, through a gate, and on to the Old Gang Smelt Mill, built about 1770 and conspicuous by its tall chimney.

Calver Hill is the backdrop to this pastoral scene, near Reeth

The remains along Old Gang Beck are particularly extensive, and include furnace houses, arches of ore hearths and a system of flues; one flue leads up to a chimney on Healaugh Crag. The flues were constructed to create a draught for the furnaces. Much of the lead fume was condensed in the flues and could be recovered, which also prevented the poisoning of animals.

Easy walking now leads onward to Surrender Bridge where the beck is crossed by an unenclosed moorland road along which some of the filming of the Herriot television series *All Creatures Great and Small* took place.

Stay on the north side of the beck, and follow a sign-posted path above the Surrender Smelt Mill and on through heather to the edge of steep-sided Cringley Bottom, a narrow ravine with enough room lower down for a couple of discretely placed tents.

Cross the ravine and climb to a stile at the wall above, and onto an improving path above enclosure walls. With no difficulty the path runs on to Thirns Farm where it branches left, ignoring a descending path to Healaugh, and climbs steeply to Moorcock Cottage before once more skirting above enclosure walls, and below Calver Hill, a shapely if modest hill.

Above the farm of Riddings keep ahead on a path across the moor to meet a wall corner, just beyond which a gate gives access to a hidden and enclosed green track, known as Skelgate. With unerring ease and superb onward views across Arkle Beck to the shattered wall of Fremington Edge, Skelgate will deliver you on to the B6270 a short way west of Reeth centre. Go left along the road to enter Reeth.

The on-going route description for the walk from Reeth now continues on page 117.

VARIANT

KELD to REETH along the River Swale
(Low level route)

Distance: 19 kilometres (11.9 miles)
Ascent: 130 metres (425 feet)

Rightly described as the Royal Road to Reeth, the low level route between Keld and Reeth is riparian loveliness at its best, an extravagance of riverside wandering across meadows lush with wild flowers. It is slightly longer than the high level route, but you would never notice!

Follow the walk from Keld as far as Crackpot Hall (described on pages 105–108), and resume the route from there.

As Crackpot Hall is approached, ignore the path climbing left, and descend, right, on a broad track continuing easily to join the River Swale below near the foot of Swinner Gill. A clear, broad path now escorts the river out towards Muker.

Approaching Ramps Holme Bridge the path forks, one branch ascending left, the other continuing ahead to the bridge. Take the path towards the bridge but, unless bound for Muker, keep on past it to another fork (both directions signposted: 'Gunnerside', though that to the left makes use of a minor roadway, and avoids the walk along the river.) Take the right branch, and continue to the right of a barn, to the first of many, very many gated (and ungated) squeeze stiles.

And on it goes: meadows, walls, barns, squeeze stiles, buttercups and daisies in a seemingly endless succession until, at the end of one pasture, the path having rejoined the Swale, leads on to a broad farm track, with a narrow riverside path dropping to the right. Take the riverside path, through the inevitable squeeze stile, until the river, and wall on the left, close the meadow down at a stile, giving onto a narrow path into woodland and above the river. At a gate the path descends once more to the riverside.

Ivelet Bridge is a fine single-arched bridge on the old corpse road from higher valley communities to Grinton, at one time the only church with hallowed ground in which to bury the dead.

Near Ivelet Bridge the river flows languorously beneath walled fields rising to the distant summit of Blea Barf. Climb, by a gate, to Ivelet Bridge.

On the bridge go left on the minor road leading to the village. At a telephone box turn right on a footpath to Gunnerside, where a minor road soon leads to a gravel path with a cottage on the left and a barn on the right. At a waymark, descend right on a narrow path through trees to a footbridge spanning Shore Gill. An exhilarating view opens up ahead of rich green pasture-land, walled fields and sturdy barns as the confines of the gill are left behind.

Once more the trail of meadows and squeeze stiles takes over until finally the path runs out onto a ledge between a fence and a steep drop to the river, soon to start descending. At a signposted track, with a low step-stile on the right, bear half-left across a field for a final flourish of meadows and stiles before entering Gunnerside through an estate of modern stone-built houses known as 'Flatlands'.

Cross the road at Gunnerside and the bridge oppo-site, to reach the King's Head Hotel. Turn right in front of the pub (on a path leading to toilets); immediately before the toilet block turn left through a gated stile into meadowland for the now familiar arrangement of stiles and meadows to reach the Swale once more just as it loops up towards the road.

A signpost on the riverbank directs walkers up a broad track to meet the road at a gate, imme-diately leaving it again by a step-stile

continued on
page 116

into woodland. For a short distance follow a narrow path high above the river to which it soon begins a steep and slippery descent, rejoining the riverbank at a stile. The path now continues along the top of flood banks flanked by a variety of trees – ash, holly, beech and sycamore – where projecting tree roots and the occasional remains of old fence posts make passage a little awkward in wet conditions. Eventually the path is forced back to the road which it is then obliged to follow until it can be left by a gate on the right.

Now follow a broad green track as it swings round

to a squeeze stile, passing outside a walled enclosure, and by means of narrow green path following the edge of a field to cross a fence by a stile. For a while stay with a field boundary and then head left across the middle of the meadow, towards a spot known as The Isles, where the path approaches the riverbank once more, a suitable spot for a brief halt, to watch the antics of oystercatchers, dippers, grey wagtails and sand martins.

A small flight of steps goes up to a stile giving on to Isles Bridge. Go a few paces left on the road to a footpath (signposted: 'Reeth') which passes briefly along the top of a wall. Follow this round to join more flood banks, and later climb on top of a narrower wall with a drop to pastureland on one side and the river on the other – no place for anyone without a good sense of balance.

On finally quitting the wall the path rejoins the riverbank for a long and delightful trek to Reeth, finally escaping from the riverbank by a steep and slippery series of zigzags through scrubby Feetham Wood, following a signposted and waymarked footpath to join the road.

Go right along the road, dodging traffic for a little over one-and-a-half kilometres (about a mile), until it can be left at a footpath sign near a small parking area on the right. The path is overgrown for a short distance, following a fence on the left, the river on the right, then at a stile it reaches the end of the meadow. Here it is necessary to ford the in-flowing Barney Beck, something that can be awkward after rain, before continuing along the wooded banks of the river.

Finally the low level route enters Reeth by a green

path passing but not using a footbridge over the Swale, leading to an enclosed path. At the top of the enclosed path bear right, coming soon, at the first houses, onto a metalled back road. Follow this and, as it bends left (signposted), continue to the centre of Reeth, to meet the B6270.

The on-going description for the main line walk continues below.

REETH

Once the centre of extensive mining activity, Reeth stands perched on a green plateau from which its shops, inns and cottages gaze out across the luxurious vale it commands. The village was established as a forest edge settlement, near the confluence of the River Swale and its most important tributary Arkle Beck, indeed the Old English meaning of the village's name is 'at the stream'. Holding such a strategic position, Reeth has, in recent times, acquired the title of capital of Mid Swaledale.

By the early nineteenth century, Reeth had developed into a thriving town, expanded by a long history

Lush farmland on the approach to Reeth

A renowned venue for numerous local fairs, agricultural shows and festivals, Reeth is a place to come back to, and a logical place for an overnight halt.

of lead mining, in much the same way Cleator grew at the behest of the iron ore industry along the Cumberland coastal fringe. But it was, perhaps surprisingly, for a place commonly associated with harsh and rough forms of employment, almost as much as the villagers aptitude for producing hand-knitted gloves, stockings and sailor caps, that helped the town to develop. People knitted whenever they could, to increase their family incomes, but the activity died out when machinery replaced the traditional needles, and men began to wear long trousers instead of breeches and stockings. This evocative aspect of life in Swaledale is explained in absorbing fashion in the Swaledale Folk Museum hidden away near a corner of the village green.

Reeth to Richmond

Distance: 16.5 kilometres (10.3 miles)
Ascent: 335 metres (1100 feet)

Marrick Priory was a twelfth-century Benedictine priory, occupied by nuns from 1154 until Henry VIII had his way with it, after which it →

Walkers who have taken the high route from Keld to Reeth will find the next section, to Richmond, a complete and surprising contrast. The River Swale and its wooded valley is never far distant, and the whole journey threaded with variety and interest all the way: an old priory, two lovely, peaceful villages, and a landscape of limestone escarpments, copses, rich meadows and leafy becks serve as a perfect balance to the scars of industry recently left behind. Those who travelled the valley route, enjoying the lush richness of the English countryside at its best, will find their appetites even further indulged here.

This is a day for relaxing, and any plans to push on beyond the Richmond area would be rendering a disservice to a most pleasant section of the walk.

It is possible to plod on along the road from Fremington to Marrick Priory, but this completely ignores a splendid opportunity to rejoin the Swale; one that makes a far more satisfying, and safer, start to the day than dodging traffic.

Leave Reeth at the southern end of the village square and follow the road to cross the bridge over the Swale. A short distance away, at a wicket gate on the right, a signpost indicates a path to Grinton. Take this to rejoin the river for a short while, then move slightly away from it on a green path across pastureland as far as Grinton Bridge.

Approaching Grinton Bridge note the impressive form of Grinton Lodge high on the moors above. Once a shooting lodge, it is now a youth hostel.

← became a ruin, with only the tower remaining. Later it was to become the parish church and a separate farm. In the late 1960s, the priory buildings were converted into an outdoor education and residential centre. It is not open to visitors, though you are allowed to have a look around the grounds.

continued on page 120

Cross the road at the bridge, and rejoin the riverbank on the other side. Reluctantly, the path soon has to leave the river, rising to join the metalled access road to Marrick Priory. Go right, along the road, a simple and meandering stroll, with the priory ahead, beckoning from its verdant surrounds.

Near the priory entrance a track crosses a cattle grid, reaching within a few paces a gate and stile on the left (signposted: 'Marrick'). Follow this path to a bench at the entrance to Steps Wood from where the retrospective view frames distant Reeth among branches of a nearby tree.

119

Go through the gate and enter Steps Wood, climb easily on a paved way, known as the Nuns Causeway or Nunnery Steps, linking the priory and Marrick village. On leaving Steps Wood, follow the path along the edge of a few fields, through gates, to reach a converted Wesleyan chapel at the entrance to Marrick. Follow the lane ahead and at a junction (signposted) bear right, continuing to a T-junction, near a telephone box. Turn right here to another junction (noting the interesting sundial on a nearby cottage, its usefulness marred by the proximity of a telegraph pole and its radiating wires). At the junction again go right, following the lane (a dead end) past the old school

Grinton Bridge

shortly to turn left (signposted) up a rough green lane leading to a series of stiles across brief fields.

The path skirts dilapidated sheds and rusting farm equipment, gently climbing all the time, until, at its highest point the fields broaden, a more satisfying vista opens up ahead and the route begins a steady descent to a broad track serving Nun Cote Nook Farm.

At the track go right, through a gate, and almost immediately left (signposted), continuing across broad meadowlands to the charmingly renovated cottage at Ellers. Pass around Ellers and cross Ellers Beck by a footbridge, then slanting up the next two fields to reach a gate near the access track to Hollins Farm.

> Beyond Hollins Farm, **Hutton's Monument**, a towering obelisk in view for some while, commemorates Matthew Hutton, a member of the once influential family that lived at Marske Hall.

Follow the track right for a short distance, and then, without entering Hollins Farm, go left, skirting a small copse to a stile. Cross the next field to a wall, and follow the wall left and, just as it enters a confined pathway, use a gate on the right to cross the ensuing field diagonally to gain the once-important road linking Reeth to

Grassy Ways on the approach to St Giles' Farm

Richmond, there descending steeply, right, into Marske village.

> **Marske** lies in an insignificant side valley of the Swale, a delightful retreat quietly going about its own business, where, it seems, only the tread of walkers disturbs the peace. The grounds of nearby Marske Hall add much to the village's natural loveliness, while the twelfth-century church of St Edmund is worth a moment's pause.
>
> The Huttons were the dominant family at Marske Hall for many years, producing two Archbishops of York, but, as W. Riley mentions in *The Yorkshire Pennines of the North–West* (1934), 'The dale has bred men of another kidney besides bishops.' His grandfather used to tell of 'the carryings-on there used to be in the big houses in his day, when the gentry wouldn't let their guests leave the table till they were too drunk to walk upstairs to bed; and the common folk were just as bad – mad on cock-fighting and coursing.'

Go down the road, amid splendid scenery, especially the view northwards of the upper valley of Marske Beck, and passing on the right the monumental grounds of Marske Hall. Near the river, at a meeting of roads, go left, over Marske Bridge and uphill to a T-junction near the Post Office.

Turn right at the junction and continue along the road for about 600m/yds until by a stile on the right access can be gained to a series of fields crossed by a narrow path that later drops to cross the wooded Clapgate Beck by a footbridge. A prominent path then slants upwards to a conspicuous cairn which turns out to be on an access track leading to West Applegarth Farm, and passes beneath the limestone cliffs of Applegarth Scar.

Continue to, and around, West Applegarth Farm to a barn ahead and a little to the right. Drop down, right, slightly towards the barn and go through a narrow gate near a wall corner. a crudely-painted signpost here suggests you are heading for the 'Costa del Sol', while the reverse direction is making for the 'Costa Brava'.

Keep on past the barn to another stile and then across a field to reach the access track to Low Applegarth Farm. Cross straight over this to the next stile, pass close by High Applegarth, and so gain the road leading to East Applegarth. Before long, however, leave the road at a stile on the left to cross a pasture well above the farm. At a stile just above East Applegarth the path meets a rough track climbing from the farm, and this is followed through a rough, untidy landscape to enter Whitcliffe Wood.

> Popular as a local walk, **Whitcliffe Wood** and the nearby Scar have a relaxing air about them, a winding-down opportunity as Richmond is approached. This whole stretch, through the seemingly endless Applegarth Farms is a haven of quiet retreat, perched high above the Swale. It is here, as the route crosses Deep Dale, that the Yorkshire Dales National Park, which has been with us since Nine Standards Rigg, is finally left.

On leaving Whitcliffe Wood, a broad track runs on to High Leases, soon to become a metalled road (Westfields) leading down, directly into Richmond. Before long it is possible to go through one of a number of low stiles on the right at the top edge of West Field for a parallel, but easier underfoot, descent to the town, either returning to Westfields, or continuing to the bottom corner of the field to meet the Reeth road (A6108) on the edge of town.

This long descending approach to Richmond via Westfields meets the A6108 near a corner shop and post office. Follow the main road (Victoria Road) left and continue along it as far as the Tourist Information Office, opposite the Turf Hotel. At a roundabout, go right, into Kings Street, which leads to the cobbled Market Place, at the centre of which stands Holy Trinity Church.

> Since Richmond is regarded by common consent as the gateway to the Dales, it follows that this section – Into the Dales – has here come to an end; the Vale of Mowbray awaits.

Just north of East Applegarth, a spot known as Willance's Leap is associated with Robert Willance, a worthy citizen of Richmond who in 1606 was hunting on horseback on the tops when mist descended. In his haste to get home he missed his way and contrived to spur his horse over the cliff edge. In the fall to the valley 200 feet below the horse was killed, but its rider surprisingly survived, although he lost a leg as a result. Willance, who lived to become an Alderman of Richmond, celebrated his deliverance by presenting the town with a silver chalice as a thanksgiving.

4. THE VALE OF MOWBRAY

Richmond, and the adjacent Vale of Mowbray, is totally dominated by its castle, as it has been since people first lived there, which almost certainly means since 1071 when the first Earl Alan of Richmond, Alan Rufus (or Alan the Red), commander of the Norman rearguard at the Battle of Hastings, received from William the Conqueror the not inconsiderable possessions of the Saxon Earl Edwin as a reward.

The name 'Richmond' comes from the French, 'Riche-mont', meaning 'strong hill', and many of its first inhabitants were of French origin, indeed skilled French workmen were brought from France to instruct local labour in castle-building techniques. With a vast inner courtyard and built on a siege-worthy scale in a commanding position, the castle was a formidable fortress, though there is little historical evidence to suggest it was ever really put to the test. Two kings of Scotland, however, William the Lion and David II, have

Richmond Castle

been imprisoned here, though there is a suggestion that at least one other was (and presumably still is) present, for legend recounts that a local man, a potter named Thompson, while seeking to escape the tongue of his nagging wife, stumbled on an entrance in the rocks beneath the castle. With peace and quiet still no doubt a strong notion in his mind he ventured in, first finding a subterranean passage, and then a huge cavern. The walls all around were hung with shields and armour, on the floor lay a number of armoured knights, while in the centre, on a raised dais, lay a regal figure grasping a sword. From his recounting of the tale, and his description of the shields, the arms of King Arthur and his knights were identified. Alas, Thompson when called upon to do so, was unable to find the entrance to the cave again. Whether this hen-pecked potter was the same man who discovered the king and his knights in a cave below the Bwlch y Saethau, near Snowdon in North Wales, whilst escaping once more from his nagging wife, is not recorded, nor indeed, what he used to drink, or in what quantities!

In similar vein is the story of how some soldiers quartered in Richmond determined to test an old tale that a secret underground passage ran from the castle to Easby Abbey. Unwilling to make the journey themselves, through long dark tunnels, with precarious roofing and foul air, they filled the head of a young drummer boy with visions of treasure and sent him into the tunnel. As the boy struggled on he rattled away at his drum, while the soldiers above ground traced its muffled sound through the streets of the town. Fainter and fainter came the sound of the drum until, near the site occupied by the former grammar school, it ceased altogether. Whether the boy ever found his treasure is not known, for he never returned. But on a quiet night you can still hear the sound of drumming, very faint and distant, coming from underground.

On a less sceptical note, Richmond's Market Place is the largest horseshoe market place in England, and was once the outer bailey of the castle; it was recobbled in 1771 when Matthew and Mark Topham were paid sixpence a yard to find stones and set them in place. How far they looked for their stones is open to debate for the present-day obelisk is on the site of a medieval cross which was pulled down in the same year. Below the obelisk, incidentally, is a reservoir holding 12,000 gallons of water, which was piped into the town; a water supply pipe, circa 1782, will be passed on the way out of town.

The Chapel of Holy Trinity, which stands in the centre of the Market Place, was founded in 1135. It has been altered and repaired many times, and has seen service as a court, prison and school; today it is the

Obelisk, Richmond

Regimental Museum of the Green Howards, the County Regiment of the old North Riding of Yorkshire.

For walkers doing their best to escape towns and cities for a while, there are opportunities to by-pass Richmond (crossing the Swale to Hudswell, for example), but really the town and its feeling of saturated antiquity is altogether too good to miss. And though the castle dominates, there is below its towering walls a labyrinthine network of narrow alleyways and back streets, 'wynds', formed by groups of quaint, haphazard buildings that would give modern planners apoplexy should anyone submit a planning application to build today in the same style. Throw in the Culloden Tower, built in 1746 to mark the defeat of Bonnie Prince Charlie by the Duke of Cumberland, and the odd folly or two, and the whole town becomes an open air museum of the grandest kind, and a tribute to those people of Richmond who have helped preserve the town and its unique character down through centuries.

The Vale of Mowbray is the northerly extension of the Vale of York, an interlude that is almost wholly agricultural in nature. It is largely flat, and, at Danby Wiske, reaches the lowest point of the walk away from the coasts; easy walking abounds, much of it skirting around and across farm fields.

Though undoubted pleasures await those who enjoy high level walking as they cross the Cleveland Hills, I can think of no valid reason, other than shortage of time, for rushing across the vale: it is a marathon crossing, a forced march that will jade the edges of your energy the next day, when, presumably, what is needed is fitness and a keen mind to appreciate fully what the Hills and the North York Moors have to offer. The low-lying land, barleyed fields, quiet farms and rural scenery of the vale are, in any case, valuable, diet-balancing ingredients of the Coast to Coast feast, and should not be gobbled indecently.

There is growing evidence, too, that many walkers agree with this view, and, having trekked from Richmond to Danby Wiske, then extend the next day a short distance from the designated route to spend the night at Osmotherly. Others reorganise the journey from Reeth to continue through Richmond and on to Bolton-on-Swale for the night, then continuing to Osmotherly the next day. If you are doing the whole crossing, the distance from Richmond to Ingleby Cross is 36.2 kilometres (22.5 miles), and the ascent 170 metres (560 feet).

Richmond to Bolton-on-Swale

Distance: 11.2 kilometres (7 miles)
Ascent: 70 metres (230 feet)

Cross the Market Place and descend via New Street and Bridge Street to reach Richmond Bridge.

En route you will find the water supply pipe, an antiquated street lamp, and, near The Green, another sundial on a wall. The Green was once an industrial suburb of Richmond, the 'rough' quarter it has been described. Here there used to be a tannery, dyeworks, corn mill, fulling mill and brewery.

Richmond Bridge dates from 1788–89, and was built by two different contractors, one operating for Richmond Corporation and the other for the county council. It spans the Swale, which from its exuberant, fast flowing youth high above Keld has grown to full stature, slower and more mature as it sets out across the farmlands of the Vale of York to join the River Ure, and so become the Ouse.

Cross the bridge and shortly turn left into playing

fields. Keep left and follow the edge of the field, with the ramparts of the castle towering high above, to enter woodland and climb to enter another field at a stile. Follow a green path going left, and as this starts to descend, locate a stile on the right by which the route passes between two scruffy barns to gain a paved way in front of a row of houses (Priory Villas).

At the end of the houses keep ahead and slightly left to join the main road (A6136). Turn right, and follow the road until, at a sharp bend and just after crossing in-flowing Sand Beck, the route goes left (signposted) to take a metalled service road leading to the sewage works, which contrasts rather sharply with the ruins of Easby Abbey across the Swale, though the view of them is rather obscured by undergrowth.

At the sewage works, skirt around the boundary on a clear path, for an odoriferous five minutes, that leads to a stile entering woodland. A muddy path treks on through the woodland, crosses a footbridge, and finally climbing to escape from the trees and undergrowth not far from the ruins of Hagg Farm.

Press on past the ruins along a narrow trod through undergrowth, and then by an improving path climb an easy brow before aiming across the next field to a stile in the far corner. Descend along a field boundary (left), and in the next field aim a quarter right on a narrow path to reach a concealed stile on the edge of more woodland. In company with a small stream continue to a driveway leading into, and through, the hamlet of Colborn, crossing a bridge and passing a pub before coming to a lane end.

Easby Abbey was founded in 1152 for a group of Premonstratensian Canons, last encountered at Shap Abbey; its rather more substantial remains are also open to the public.

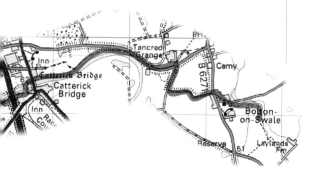

Catterick Bridge, more or less as we now see it, was commissioned by seven local gentry in 1422, and built by three stonemasons each of whom put their stonemason's mark on the stones of the old bridge. The bridge took three years to build, at a total cost of £173 6s 8d.

As the lane bends right, keep ahead through a gate and turn sharp right to approach a farmyard. Once in the farmyard go left and follow a broad track along the edge of a pasture, later going left along another field boundary to a stile.

Now continue to the right above Colburn Beck Wood and the unseen Swale. Two gates lead into a gently rising pasture towards St Giles Farm.

Nearby is the site of **St Giles Hospital**, one of many run under monastic orders, though there is little to see on the ground from the route. The site was excavated as recently as 1990 and revealed a large quantity of skeletons that were all removed to York for further research.

Do not enter St Giles Farm, but, as the access gate is approached, go left on a developing path to meet its access track at a stile. Only a short while later, just after a cattle grid, go left along a field boundary, crossing the boundary path at a stile about half way down the field. Now a path continues along the top of the bank above the Swale, becoming muddy as it approaches a field access track serving Thornbrough Farm. On reaching the farm look for a path (unclear) descending left to the point where the Swale, and our path, passes under the A1. If the path is missed, simply follow the farm access out, and, as it bends right, descend sharply left (waymarked).

Pass under the noisy A1, and press on, keeping straight ahead, to pass beneath a defunct metal railway bridge, shortly beyond which the path rises slightly to the right to reach the A6136 (the old A1), opposite Catterick racecourse, with Catterick Bridge on the left.

Beside the bridge, the **Bridge House Hotel**, also built in more spacious days, has a style and charm often lacking in these later days of mechanisation and standardisation; its atmosphere and tradition date back to the old coaching days. In such a strategic position, coast to coast, it is not surprising that it welcomes walkers. In 1442, the hotel was known as the George and Dragon, and was an important coaching halt between London and Scotland. Until 1950 the present hotel was owned by the Lawsons of Brough Hall, Catterick.

The area around the hotel has great historical interest, dating from the time when Catterick Bridge was a Brigantian city, then known as 'Cherdarich', meaning 'the camp by the water'. When the Romans arrived they extended the city into a great military centre, and Dere Street, the main Roman road to the north, forded the river at Catterick Bridge. The Romans renamed the area 'Cataractonium'.

Cross the road with care, and go left over the bridge, following the abutments round, right, to a squeeze stile giving access to a meadow. Follow the Swale pleasantly until, as it approaches gravel works, a path ascends left to the B6271.

There is a moment of some sadness here, for, as our steps now head for the road, we bid farewell to the Swale. In all its moods, it has been our companion for many a mile since we first met it near Keld; now, quietly it slips away to join the Ure, and though a while longer it remains there, in the distance, we never again tramp its banks. So, does not such charming company deserve at least a moment's thought as we take our leave?

View across pastured fields to Bolton-on-Swale

Turn right along the road, and at the first turning on the right (signposted) go down a concrete road. Take the first left (also signposted), a broad track leading soon to Bolton-on-Swale.

At the end of the track the route meets the B6271 again, going right for a short distance, and then left, near the village pump, to head for the church, St Mary's.

St Mary's church is a delightful structure, its clock tower constructed of exquisitely-hued sandstone blacks. But the principal feature of interest here is the monument in the churchyard dedicated to one Henry Jenkins, whose claim to fame was that from his birth at nearby Ellerton in the year 1500 he lived to be 169, dying at Ellerton in 1670. The monument is a fitting tribute to the man, even if the mason did rather miscalculate his word spacing – Oh, what would he have given for a word processor and proportional spacing, I wonder?

Bolton-on-Swale to Danby Wiske

Distance: 11 kilometres (6.9 miles)
Ascent: 35 metres (115 feet)

Between Bolton-on-Swale and Danby Wiske the route uses a succession of farmed fields to link these two charming villages. In some spots, especially close by farms, the going underfoot is less than ideal, but the onward route throughout, is always waymarked.

If you need to make haste, it is possible to hoof it along the quiet back road from Ellerton Hill, via Streetlam, to Danby Wiske, though this holds no appeal beyond speed of

St Mary's Church,
Bolton-on-Swale

passage and uniformity of going underfoot. It is detailed below as a variant.

At St Mary's Church go left along the lane to a stile on the right, after a large building in private grounds. In the ensuing field follow a path, left, which escorts lazy Bolton Beck round the field edge and by way of intermittent stiles to a dilapidated stone bridge. Cross the bridge and continue downstream, past a useless wooden gate, and on to meet the access track to Layland's Farm. Cross the farm track and the next field to a stile onto a lane at Ellerton Hill.

Walkers wanting to use the variant route to Danby Wiske should now refer to page 136.

Go left along the minor road near Ellerton Hill, but soon leave it, going right in front of a row of houses, and continuing down past open barns to a gate. Now go ahead, following a field boundary, keeping it on the left, to another gate giving access to a corner of a field, just beyond which a further gate lets you on to the B6271.

Follow the road, left, for about one kilometre (half a mile) to a sharp bend with trees on both sides of the road. Here, as the road bends away, go left, through two gates, on a broad bridleway leading eventually to residential property. Keep ahead, past the houses, to enter an enclosed path that ends in a confontation with three gates. Go through the gate ahead, and take a path along the field margin on the right, keeping a hedgerow on the right. When the field boundaries open up for a short stretch, continue ahead, always keeping a low hedgerow on the right-hand side.

Continue to a gate, just before which a small stream is crossed, and beyond which the path switches sides, in relationship to the hedgerow. Keep ahead to Stanhowe Cottages, and press on, through a gate, once more following a field margin, until another stream is crossed. Keep ahead through a gate. At a hedge corner, with farm buildings away to the left, leave the field margin and branch obliquely right, aiming for a solitary tree and another hedge corner, beyond which a field boundary runs out to a gate, and yet another encounter with the B6271.

On leaving the field, turn sharp left, heading for Red House Farm on a public bridleway. Continue to the farm, and just after passing Moor House Farm, the path forks. Take the right branch to Moor House Farm. Keeping the farm buildings always on the left, proceed to a gate on the right, and there enter a field, following the left boundary, of walls and buildings, to a step-stile.

Cross the step-stile and go immediately left, through a gate, then heading half right, across a pasture, to another step-stile, giving onto a sleeper bridge across a small stream. Head forward across the next field to a stile and waymark, set low in a hedgerow. Cross the

Streetlam

stile, and follow the field boundary left, half circling round the field until a stile, marked by a tall white post, is located in a hedgerow. Press on to another, similar, stile. In the next field continue ahead along a field boundary, and running out to meet the road to Streetlam, near Middle Brockholme Farm.

Turn right, down the Streetlam road (i.e. away from Streetlam) for 400m/yds, and then go left on a broad track, shortly ignoring the turning to High Brockholme. Keep ahead through a number of gates, always forward, until the boundary finally swings round to the left. Go through yet another gate, turning left to be confronted by a wide gap in a hedgerow with a beckoning waymark and iron gate beyond. Ignore this, but keep right, following the hedgerow (now on the left). At the far end of the field the path reaches an enclosed pathway through hedgerows and willow scrub, finally reaching daylight again with only one last field margin to tackle before reaching the road into Danby Wiske. Go left at the road to enter the village.

Variant: *The following variant details an alternative route from Bolton-on-Swale to Danby Wiske, that is entirely road walking. Its only virtue is speed.*

Bolton-on-Swale to Danby Wiske

Distance: 10 kilometres (6.25 miles)
Ascent: 35 metres (115 feet)

Turn left now along the lane, following it through the shadowy confines of Fatten Hill and Hodber Hill Plantations to a minor crossroads. Once more go left and then immediately right towards Whitwell, to a corner, with a wooden picnic table strategically positioned for a brief halt. Now follow the road to Streetlam, a sleepy community, with the telephone box being the centrepiece!

Immediately on crossing the road at Streetlam, look for a signposted stile on the right. Cross this and go left along the field edge, avoiding the small white gate, and heading for a larger one nearby. Pass through the gate, ignore the large gap on the right, and move left, avoiding small allotments and paddocks, to follow the field boundary by numerous stiles towards West Farm. As the farm is reached a slight departure from the field hedgerow moves half-right to a stile before resuming its hedgerow-hugging progress.

Eventually the fields are left at an access track to Middle Farm. Go left here and soon rejoin the minor road leading right, down Park Hill to Danby Wiske.

The on-going route for the walk to Ingleby Cross and Osmotherly continues from here.

Danby Wiske to Ingleby Cross

Distance: 14 kilometres (8.75 miles)
Ascent: 65 metres (215 feet)

More easy rural walking ensues, taking the route to the very feet of the Cleveland Hills. This is a perfect time to relax and plod on happily in preparation for the effort that the hills and moors to come will demand. The Vale

*Setting out from
Danby Wiske*

of Mowbray may not be everyone's cup of tea, but it possesses a gentle, soothing insistence where everything is tidily in its place, birds call constantly from flower-decked hedgerows, cows peer at you inquisitively as they go about their daily munching, and all the villages are neatly trimmed and washed. It is the brief passage that prepares the way for the grand finale, the final movement.

In Danby Wiske turn right on reaching the White Swan Inn, and follow Danby Lane, soon to cross the River Wiske by a single-arched bridge; no Swale this river, but an overgrown stream with pretentions it can't live up to. Continue along this road, past Lazenby Hall, with grass verges for a while to ease the plodding. Soon the road crosses the East Coast main railway line, and continues to a small group of trees on the right, near its junction with Crowfoot Lane.

At the junction, go left (signposted) and continue to the busy A167 at Oaktree Hill. Cross the road and go

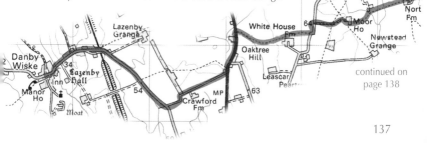

continued on
page 138

137

left until, just after Oaktree Farm (on the left), a broad track (gate and stile) leaves the road, right.

Press on along a green track flanked by hedgerows. When confronted by a number of gates, keep ahead with a low hedgerow on the right to a stile. Once across the stile a path, seasonally subdued by undergrowth, fights its way along a narrow tract of ground towards White House Farm, where it starts to improve. Without approaching the farm, continue ahead, as captivating glimpses of the Cleveland Hills appear between gaps in otherwise cloaking hedgerows. Finally, the track reaches a minor backroad, Deighton Lane, at a bend. Go left for a short distance to a farm access leading to Moor House.

Keep on between farm buildings to a gate; through the gate turn left and cross a narrow enclosure to a stile at the bottom, and then follow the field margin round to a gap on the left, and there go ahead to cross a small stream, continuing half-left across another enclosure towards the ruins of a farm.

Field margin walking near Wray House

Cross a stile near an open barn and follow a field margin away towards Northfield Farm. At the end of the field cross another stream by a narrow sleeper bridge with a stile at either end. In the large meadow that follows head directly for Northfield Farm on a well-fertilised green path, aiming a little to the left of the buildings, and locate a stile across an intermediate fence, on the left. Ahead and at a step-stile (waymarked), the path reaches a farm access. Now go left to pass round the buildings at Northfield House Farm, and there swing right to pursue the access road to its junction with Long Lane.

Long Lane is a less well known Roman Road, and here the route goes right, along its metalled surface for 200m/yds until, at a signposted farm access, it heads left and through a gate towards Wray Farm.

On reaching the farm buildings go right, down a short access track to a gate and a crude stile, with an obvious railway crossing point directly ahead. Ignore this crossing, and go sharply to the left along a hedgerow, and then head across the field, slightly right, to reach a concrete stile at a pedestrian crossing of the railway.

Once safely across the railway, traverse the field that follows to a bottom corner where there is a metalled footbridge between stiles. Cross this and in a few strides come to the corner of another field, reaching it by a small sleeper bridge spanning an overgrown ditch. Now head left along the field margin, trekking around two sides until it meets Low Moor Lane, a surfaced minor lane that takes the route on for a while, to the left, and passes close by Harlsey Grove Farm. Here go right on a rougher track to meet a metalled surface once more.

As the rough extension of Low Moor Lane meets the metalled roadway, go right for a short distance to another road, and here left, leaving it almost immediately for an access track to Sydal Lodge.

On the approach to Sydal Lodge continue ahead through a gate, keeping farm buildings on the right, and

Throughout the whole of the crossing from Danby Wiske the scenery is entirely pastoral, the land given over to agriculture, and the walking of the easiest kind with barely a gradient to be encountered anywhere. In every direction cultivated farm fields, hedgerows, and coppices stretch as far as the eye can see. The retrospective view is of the hills of Swaledale, now seeming far, far away, while ahead the Cleveland Hills are almost beneath our feet.

139

Ingleby Cross

At Ingleby Cross the route enters the North Yorkshire Moors National Park, and can be said to have engaged upon the final lap, roughly 80 kilometres (50 miles). Heather-clad moors await, extravagant scenery, wide panoramas, and, in just a few days, journey's end.

passing an open barn to a gate. Continue ahead on a narrow path across the field that follows, heading for the prominent ruins of Brecken Hill Farm. The path descends to a footbridge, once more meeting the River Wiske on its continuing and vain search for riverine excitement.

> Though never achieving more than modest, slow-moving proportions, the River Wiske nevertheless has given its name, as a suffix, to a number of villages along its meandering route. It finally gives up its search for greater glory as it meets the Swale, not far from Thirsk.

Cross the footbridge and immediately ascend a corn-field to reach Brecken Hill Farm, where, in season, a feast may be had of plums and elderberry. Keep the buildings on the left and then carry out a series of rights and lefts around field margins and along access lanes, finally to reach the A19. Cross this busy dual carriageway, linking Northallerton and Stockton-on-Tees, and follow the lane ahead to Ingleby Arncliffe. A quick left and right then lead down to Ingleby Cross.

5. THE NORTH YORK MOORS

Stretching from the outskirts of Thirsk in the west to the coast in the east, and about half that distance in a north–south direction, the North York Moors present an open, unenclosed, virtually uninhabited expanse of high moorland that seems to have been devised solely with walkers in mind. In reality the moors are not one, but a huge collection of them, almost 150, each bearing a name, though quite where one ends and the next begins is a matter for geographers and others who seek to debate such niceties.

Along the southern boundary of the Moors lies the Vale of Pickering, feeding into its companion, the Vale of Mowbray, to the west, while the northern extremities filter out as they reach Teesside. It is not by chance that the whole of this area, looking on a map not unlike the outline of Australia, has been embraced with the North York Moors National Park. It is a beautiful and true wilderness, traversed by few roads, and most of those seemingly aimless. Here grouse clatter about in the low heather where once dinosaurs and pterodactyls may

On the last leg: Whitby in the distance

have roamed, and primitive man settled at a time when climactic conditions became favourable.

Not unlike the moorlands of the Northern Pennines in character, the North York Moors are, however, rather less bleak, a touch more colourful, and with escape in an emergency a little easier to effect – though when the mist rolls in and everything is lost save for the few strides ahead of you, you may be forgiven for doubting the veracity of that observation. There is much here to please walker/naturalists, as well as geologists and industrial archaeologists, with an amazing range of fungi in particular.

Few walls of fences encroach onto these gently rolling moors, contrasting sharply with the patterned fields viewed from the northern escarpment, here known as the Cleveland Hills, where the loftiness of the vantage point also arouses sensations of great freedom and satisfaction. Not by chance is a good section of this magnificent upland also shared with two other walks of note, the Lyke Wake Walk, a gruelling 40-mile walk against the clock, and the Cleveland Way, which in 1969 became Britain's second official long distance path, all 109 miles of it: not bad for such a compact area.

Ingleby Cross to Clay Bank Top

Distance: 18.4 kilometres (11.5 miles)
Ascent: 775 metres (2545 feet)

On the last lap now, so to speak, but between Ingleby Cross and Glaisdale there are few opportunities actually along the line of the walk to find accommodation. Fortunately, many bed and breakfast proprietors with accommodation in the numerous villages that shelter beneath the Cleveland Hills and the eastern moors offer ferry services, and will pick walkers up from virtually anywhere. In some instances, this means being able to spend more than one night at a particular location, with transportation at the start and end of each day to resume the walking. Purists, of course, would never think of such a thing, but there are many advantages to it; some concern hygiene, dry clothes, comfort and warm beds, others the possibility of having a day or two with a light rucsack for a change; after all, the walk is not intended as a trial by ordeal.

The customary day's end to this section is Clay Bank Top (nearest telephone one kilometre, half a mile, off-route to the south), though the up and down nature of the stretch from Huthwaite Green at the head of Scugdale can be quite tiring. The act of extending the previous day to reach Osmotherly (a pleasant notion, albeit it with an uphill finish towards the end of the day) facilitates a more leisurely saunter to Clay Bank Top, preceded, possibly, by a visit to Mount Grace Priory.

Unless time is of pressing concern I would strongly advocate tackling these final few days at a relaxed pace. The Lake District undoubtedly has its attractions, but the North York Moors are no makeweight, possessing just as much as Lakeland to please a walker who has already travelled 140 miles and now, with confidence and determination, has the end firmly in sight.

Leave Ingleby Cross down the road at the side of the Blue Bell Inn to reach and cross the A172, so gaining a metalled road (over a cattle grid) leading to Ingleby Arncliffe Church (All Saints), a simple uncomplicated structure backed by the gables of Arncliffe Hall.

Climb easily for a while to the brow of a hill and a gate

Arncliffe Hall is a fine Georgian house, dating from 1754, and was probably built by John Carr of York.

on the left, and continue on a broad path (signposted) across a field towards Arncliffe Wood, part of the Forestry Commission's Cleveland Forest. The

continued on page 144

143

wood is entered at a gate just beyond which a T-junction is reached. Go right here and climb once more to a junction branching right to Park House, the North York Moors Adventure Centre. Unless staying overnight at Park House, or visiting Mount Grace Priory, stay left on the forest trail, progressing further into the forest.

Mount Grace Priory was founded in 1398 by Thomas Holland, Duke of Surrey and Earl of Kent, and a nephew of Richard II, though it was not completed until after 1440. Its full title is 'The House of the Assumption of the Blessed Virgin Mary and St Nicholas of Mount Grace in Ingleby', and it remains today of considerable ecclesiastical interest, one of the finest examples of an old Carthusian monastery existing anywhere.

Life in these monasteries was one we would countenance today only with abject horror. Mount Grace housed fifteen or so hermit-monks, living as solitaries in a two-storey cell, twenty-two feet square. The ground floor had a fireplace and a wooden staircase to the room above, with a small garden separated from the next by high walls, in which the monk worked alone. Meeting their fellows only for matins and vespers, and the occasional feast day when services were held in the church, the monks would spend ten hours each day in their cells, reading, praying, eating and meditating. So that no contact may be made with the server, food was brought to the monks and passed through a right-angled hatch. The monks remained at Mount Grace for 140 years, until the dissolution in 1539.

Now in the guardianship of English Heritage, the priory is generally open to the public, and contains a reconstructed and furnished cell; walkers heading no further than Clay Bank Top will find ample time in the day to divert through Arncliffe Wood to the priory where the austerity and greyness of the lives of those who lived and died there is most noticeably impressed on a receptive mind.

The path rises steadily to a T-junction; here go right, and continue to the edge of the forest at a gate, beyond which a track leads down to Osmotherly. At this point the Cleveland Way is first encountered.

Walkers heading for an overnight stay in Osmotherly should leave the forest at this point, following the Cleveland Way across fields, through three kissing gates, past Chapel Wood Farm until reaching the road leading into Osmotherly, there turning right into the village.

Osmotherly is a small, thriving village at the point where the Cleveland Way, the Lyke Wake Walk and the Coast to Coast meet. Originally, the community developed as an agricultural market village, but during the eighteenth and nineteenth centuries it was also a thriving industrial centre. Many of the houses date from these days, built in the period 1800–30 to provide accommodation for workers in the alum quarries and jet mines, and are constructed of traditional Yorkshire sandstone.

The village's name has always been a source of interest. In the Domesday Book it is recorded as 'Asmundrelac', Asmund being an Old Norse name. Later, under Anglian influence, this would corrupt to 'Osmund's Ley', a ley, like a thwaite, being a clearing, but, as ever, there is a more imaginative tale to be told.

A local princess dreamt her son, Os (or Oswy), would drown on a certain day, and so on that day ordered a nurse to take him to a safe place. Roseberry Topping, then known as Odinsberg, that prominent cone-shaped hill near Great Ayton that has been in view for a while as the Cleveland Hills were approached, seemed safe enough. Certainly, the nurse found it a safe and comforting haven for she fell asleep, allowing the baby prince to wander away. When the nurse awoke it was to find the prince lying face down in a hillside spring, dead. He was buried at Osmotherly. Later, his mother died of grief and was buried at his side, so 'Os-by-his-mother-lay'. Chronologically, it doesn't tie up, of course; perhaps the village should be 'Mother-by-Os-ley'! It is all highly improbable, but nice.

Continuing from the forest edge, the main route does not leave the forest, but doubles back, signposted: 'Cleveland Way', as are most of the signposts for the next few miles. Climb away from the gate on a clear path through South Wood. At the top of the wood the path escorts a wall to a Radio Station, squeezing then between the station and the wall to approach the summit of Beacon Hill, with the first wide-ranging views of the Cleveland Plain now coming into view.

The trig point on the summit of Beacon Hill officially marks the start of the **Lyke Wake Walk**. These days the walk begins from the Lyke Wake Stone on a little mound opposite the first car park at the eastern end of Cod Beck Reservoir. It is a 40-mile walk across the moors, and must be completed within 24 hours.

Continue away from the top of Beacon Hill to arrive at a gate, giving access to Scarth Wood Moor. A few metres ahead the path forks. The branch on the left closely follows the boundary of Scarth Wood, while the onward route lies by the right branch, an open track across the heather-clad moor.

Scarth Wood Moor like most of the moors that make up the North York Moors, is of considerable prehistoric significance, and has a number of Bronze Age 'barrow', or grave mounds. Geologically, it is affected by three faults, the largest being that along the line of Scarth

Nick, soon to be encountered, and originally formed by an overflow of meltwater from a huge glacier that once filled Scugdale.

When the path rejoins a wall (the handiwork of a Community Programme Team working here in 1988), a waymark for the Lyke Wake Walk ('LWW') is soon reached. Here go left and descend to Scarth Nick, following the wall, and ignoring more prominent tracks heading off to the right.

At Scarth Nick, reached by two flights of steps that do nothing for your knees, go left along the metalled roadway to cross a cattle grid, and then head right, at a stile, into forest.

Scarth Nick also marks the crossing point of the Hambleton Drove Road, one of numerous routes taken by the tough, weather-beaten Scottish cattlemen, hired to drive cattle from Scotland into England, to sell at various market towns, even as far south as London.

When these drove roads were regularly in use it was a busy time for sheep and cattle farmers, the Industrial Revolution of the late eighteenth and early nineteenth centuries aggravating an already growing demand for beef that could not be met by the English farmers. Ironically, it was the Industrial Revolution, and the invention of steam power, that sealed the fate of cattle drovers, as steam power overcame leg power, and the new railway network made it possible to slaughter cattle locally and send carcasses to markets by rail. Declining rapidly by 1850, at the turn of the century droving had ceased altogether, turning into the pages of history days when, as Dorothy Wordsworth recalls in her journal, 'the sun shone hot, [and] the little Scottish cattle panted and tossed fretfully about.'

The path through the wood soon joins a forest trail, where the walk continues ahead along level ground. At a break in the forest on the left (splendid view over the village of Swainby below), leave the forest trail and descend steeply, left, down a wide track. At a junction

The Lyke Wake Walk began with an article in *The Dalesman* in August 1955, with the first challenge being taken up on the 1st October 1955. Those first challengers, who included Bill Cowley, instigator of the walk, 'cheered each other on by reciting the Lyke Wake Dirge.' Normally sung at funerals in the seventeenth century 'by the vulgar people in Yorkshire', the dirge suggests that everyone, after death, must make a journey over a wide and difficult moor. Those who have done good deeds in their life – given away food and drink, silver and gold, written helpful guidebooks (?) – will receive aid and will cross the moor safely. But if not, the luckless soul will sink into Hell flames, or Rosedale bog!

Ice sheets have advanced and retreated over the British landscape at least four times in the last two million years, a period of alternating warm and cold climactic conditions known as the Great Ice Age, which effectively refrigerated everything. The last period, known as the Devensian, did not end until about 10,000 years ago, when plants began to recolonise the moors, animals returned, and prehistoric people appeared on the scene.

go left and immediately right (signposted) before a gate. A good, hardcore path continues round the edge of Clain Wood, and when this ends take a stile on the left into a field. A rough track heads across the field to a ford (and footbridge) at Piper Beck, beyond which a narrow lane leads left, across Scugdale Beck, and passes Hollin Hill Farm to a T-junction at Huthwaite Green.

Cross the road here to a gate to the right of a telephone box (the last chance to phone for accommodation/pick up before Clay Bank Top), and take the enclosed path leading uphill towards Live Moor Plantation. At a gate and stile we step outside the plantation boundary, following a fence round a stile to re-enter the forest below a steep flight of steps clambering upwards to Live Moor. Keep across a forest trail to a final stile giving access to the open moor. There is little respite from the uphill toil, as the path tackles the shoulder of Round Hill, until, at last, it finds a contour and lopes off energetically in the direction of distant Carlton Moor.

> Now, really for the first time, the undulating skyline of the Cleveland Hills stretches out ahead; an enticing, exciting prospect, custom made, one might think, for walkers.

From Live Moor the way ahead is not in doubt, an easy descent being made before the broad path leads steadily upwards, skirting Gold Hill and the edge of Faceby Bank to plod on to the broad expanse of Carlton Moor.

> The presence on Carlton Moor of a broad strip of bare ground may puzzle for a while, especially if visibility is not good. This is the runway of a glider station, a barren, desert-like landscape, strewn with small rocks that seem to offer little prospect of a smooth landing.

Sandwiched between this 'runway' and the escarpment edge, the path continues uneventfully to the summit of Carlton Moor, marked by a trig pillar and a boundary stone.

Below the moor top, and shortly to be encountered, are some old jet mine workings. **Jet** in this region is synonymous with Whitby, though the history of jet mining and jet jewellery is much more ancient, beads of the light, fossilised wood having been discovered in Bronze Age burial mounds dating from 2500 to 3500 years ago. Jet was formed about 130 million years ago when pieces of coniferous driftwood became buried by Jurassic sea mud.

In more recent times it was a retired naval captain who introduced two Whitby men to the art of turning on a lathe, leading to the production, around 1800 onwards, of beads and crosses; by 1850 there were over fifty workshops in Whitby alone. Even so, jet would never have received the prominence it did had not Queen Victoria taken to wearing it as Court mourning following the death of Prince Albert. It was already generally recognised as an emblem of mourning, but with royal patronage a boom period followed, and those fifty workshops quadrupled in number, giving employment eventually to over 1400 men and boys. Though the fashion ultimately declined, jet is still carved in Whitby, and may be found by diligent searching on the beaches there.

Alum Crystals, too, were a product of this remarkable region, with at least twenty-five quarries active between 1600 and 1871, and Nature has not yet finished her work of disguising the massive shale heaps that litter Carlton Bank, and other places. The value of alum lay in its property as a fixative of dyes in cloth, a secret process mastered throughout Italy in the sixteenth century, and, towards the end of that century, by a member of the Chaloner family in Britain. Requiring 50 to 100 tons of shale to produce one ton of alum crystals, its quarrying was a pick and shovel nightmare for the poorly-paid labourers involved in the long, tedious process of extraction. Once won from the earth, the shale, piled in large mounds, had to be burned slowly for up to a year, before soaking in water. Then the solution had to be boiled, crystallised and purified, a process that required scrub for the burning, water for soaking, coal for the boiling, seaweed and human urine for the chemistry, an altogether messy and protracted

For reasons I am unable to comprehend, the boundary stone, on the 3rd October 1992, was the venue of a lady-birds' convention; more than sixty specimens were present, ranging over at least five (to my untrained eye) noticeably different species, gathered singly and in groups, sheltering in the shallow hollows and niches of the boundary stone.

way of going about business that came to a halt in 1871, with the closure of the Kettleness and Boulby works.

The onward trail from the summit of Carlton Moor picks a cautious and re-routed way down Carlton Bank, along the edge of old alum quarries, and through large waste heaps of burnt shale.

On reaching an access road, near forest plantations, go left at a signpost to meet a metalled roadway at a gate. Turn right along the road for a short distance, leaving it by a stile on the left to begin the ascent to Cringle Moor by a green path leading to Lord Stones Café, an unexpected and welcome treat hidden beneath a raised embankment (toilets and information centre here).

Perhaps the café should go by the name 'Lords' Stone', since such a stone, known as the Three Lords' Stone, stands nearby on the former parish boundary. It commemorates the Lords of the time, Duncombe of Helmsley (now Feversham), Marwood of Busby Hall, and Ailesbury, the latter at that time holding Scugdale.

The route now follows a path, passing a small copse, to a wall corner just beyond which a stile gives access to a broad green track, part of a footpath renovation scheme started in 1991. A short pull ensues to the nab of Cringle Moor, at Cringle End, where a view indicator, a welcome stone seat and a boundary stone await.

The stone seat was erected in memory of Alec Falconer (alias 'Rambler'), a founder member of the Middlesbrough Rambling Club, who died in 1968. He promoted the notion of a long distance walk along the hills and coastline of the North York Moors, but, sadly, he died a year before the Cleveland Way was opened.

The onward path keeps to the escarpment edge above Kirby Bank, before descending steeply through a spill of boulders, stones and mining debris to the broad col before Cold Moor. From the col follow a wall (on the right) along a Land Rover track to reach a stream bed. At this point a path crosses the stream and continues ahead along the boundary of Broughton Plantation ultimately to arrive at Clay Bank Top by a sheltered and rather more level passage. The main line, however, goes right, just before the stream, at a gate and stile to follow a dilapidated wall ahead and then left, passing through a gate, before continuing to the top of the moor.

The summit of Cold Moor is marked by a modest sandstone cairn, and is followed by a short walk along an escarpment edge, descending to Garfit Gap, at a gate. Continue ahead along the line of a collapsed wall, passing through to gaps in lateral walls. A final short pull leads to the Wainstones, a tumble of boulders and rock outcrops that represents one of only a small number of rock climbing opportunities in the North York Moors. Various paths weave a way through the Wainstones, beyond which easy walking leads on across the plateau of Hasty Bank. Stay with the edge of Hasty Bank's escarpment (a pleasant prospect) before tackling the inevitable steep descent to the top of a plantation and wall corner (stile), from there following the wall down to meet the B1257 Stokesley–Helmsley road at Clay Bank Top, more correctly known as 'Hagg's Gate'.

> Throughout the whole of this lengthy traverse the highlight has been the superb views northwards and the dramatic escarpment dropping to forestry and farmland below, while the pinnacles of the Wainstones provide a stark contrast to the luxurious vegetation that has patterned the journey from Ingleby Cross.
>
> Clay Bank Top is an idyllic spot. The bluebell woods of Ingleby Bank stand on one side, with Bilsdale stretching far away on the other. It is here that walkers will need to decide what to do for the night. Those with tents on their backs will have no problem finding a suitable pitch before too long, but others seeking their creature comforts may be dependent on a pick up service.

The highest point of Cringle Moor is **Drake Howe**, a Bronze Age burial mound, and the second highest point on this crossing of the Cleveland Hills. Its summit is set back from the path, and as a result is the only summit along this stretch that is not visited.

Clay Bank Top to Glaisdale
(Beggar's Bridge)

Distance: 27.25 kilometres (17 miles)
Ascent: 310 metres (1015 feet)

With nothing more than a short pull onto Urra Moor to cause any exertion, the walk to Glaisdale, perhaps longer than some might like, is surprisingly effortless, for quite a long time following the line of the old Rosedale mineral railway, and providing the fastest section of the whole walk. Very few signs of civilisation will be encountered along this stretch until the Lion Inn at Blakey Ridge, and nothing beyond that until Glaisdale is reached.

From Clay Bank Top the walk continues to the highest point on the North York Moors, Botton Head on Urra Moor. Go through the roadgate, keeping along a stone wall that marks the boundary of the medieval Greenhowe deer park, and following an ancient pack-horse track once much used by smugglers. Initially the track climbs energetically, through a narrow cleft in a rocky barrier before reaching a gate and there gaining access to the open moor of Carr Ridge.

From this point the walking is of the easiest kind, with wide-ranging views across a landscape of constantly changing colours, seen at its vibrant best in early autumn when the heather is in full bloom and the sun and clouds combine to provide a limitless number of lighting variations to enhance the scene. This is perhaps the finest stretch in the North York Moors, but potentially the most lethal in poor visibility. The great moor, badly damaged by fire in the 1930s and only now recovering, has some deceiving contours, which may be one of the reasons why the Justices sitting in Northallerton in 1711 decreed that guideposts should be erected throughout the North Riding of Yorkshire (as it then was). Opposite the trip point on the top of Urra Moor stands one such guidepost, the *Hand Stone*, with a rough carving on each side depicting a hand and inscribed with the words 'This is the way to Stoxla' (Stokesley), and 'This is the way to Kirbie' (Kirkbymoorside). A short way further on, and probably much older, stands the *Face Stone*, depicting a crude face incised on its east side.

From the top of Urra Moor a broad track begins an easy descent to a spot known as Bloworth Crossing, there the onward route joins the embankments of the former Rosedale Ironstone Railway. At a line of grouse butts on the left, ignore a faint green path going left, but keep ahead instead to a slight boggy depression, climbing easily to the railway embankment. On reaching the trackbed, turn right, and follow this literally all the way to the Lion Inn (roughly 8 kilometres: 5 miles) at the head of Blakey Ridge, a long serpentine walk of the easiest kind.

At a second gate shortly after Bloworth Crossing the route

The Rosedale Ironstone Railway was constructed in 1861 to carry iron from Rosedale over the watershed to the furnaces of Teesside. Iron Age man more than likely worked the Rosedale iron ore, but in 1328 Edward III granted land for that purpose to the nuns of Rosedale Abbey. Five centuries later the ore was dismissed as poor quality and worthless, only for it to be regarded later still as magnetic ore of the highest quality. Once the railway link was made across the moors some five millions tons were extracted in the first twenty years. By the later 1920s, →

continued on page 154

takes its leave of the Cleveland Way, but is not yet able to shake off the Lyke Wake Walk, which continues with us for some time yet. For some distance the railway bed contours neatly around the head of Farndale, a

← however, the seams
had worn thin and a
depression was
looming, presaging the
final end of the mining
operations.

wild and beautiful valley, renowned for its springtime
display of daffodils, and once destined to be flooded to
supply water to Hull, until common sense prevailed over
insensitive bureaucracy.

After what seems like an eternity, the Lion Inn at
Blakey Junction springs encouragingly into view, rather
like an oasis after the trackless way of the disused
mineral railway. As it is approached, the trackbed is left
to pursue a muddy path leading up towards the inn
(signposted: 'LWW').

> Say goodbye at this point to the old railway; in its own
> right it is, if you like, an ancient monument, a testament
> to hard-working men now long forgotten. We shall see
> it again soon, circling the head of Rosedale, but when
> at Blakey Ridge we step off it, its companionship and
> speedy passage are finally gone from beneath our feet.
> A moment's pause and a silent word of gratitude for the
> men who, unwittingly, made part of our journey easy
> and comfortable to follow, would not go amiss.

The path follows a wall on the right towards the inn,
coming first to a raised circular mound, Blakey Howe,
an ancient burial mound used in more recent

times for cockfighting. Here, without
continuing to the inn, unless staying there
overnight or in search of intermediate refreshment, go left
at the mound to reach the road between Hutton-le-Hole
to the south and Castleton and Westerdale to the north.

Head left along the road, which has ample grassy
verges, high above Rosedale and its river, the Seven.
Opposite a large boundary stone on the left, which has
acquired the name Margery Bradley, a path branches

right across the head of Rosedale to meet the Rosedale Abbey road near an ungainly white-painted cross, known, for obvious reasons, as Fat Betty. This shortcut is messy and saves little in time: a better alternative is to stay on the road.

Moorland Crosses are a prominent and frequent occurrence on the North York Moors; there are more than thirty named crosses on the moors, probably a larger collection than anywhere else in Britain. Though many have attracted independent names, they are nevertheless a symbol of Christ's death, and first appeared on the moors during the seventh-century growth of Christianity in the region.

The prevalence, and significance, of these moorland crosses was, in 1974, given a measure of official blessing when one of them, **Ralph Cross** at the head of Rosedale and more or less central to the moors, was used as the emblem of the North York Moors National Park Authority.

By omitting the path between Margery Bradley and Fat Betty, keeping instead to the road for a while longer, Ralph Cross will be encountered a short distance beyond the Rosedale Abbey turning, a choice of route that will cause no hardship, and which will be found more acceptable underfoot than cutting corners needlessly.

From Fat Betty continue along the road for a short distance until a string of boundary stones going left marks the line of a possible shortcut, saving all of 100m/yds. This shortcut, if taken, brings the route back to the road for a minute or so, before another narrow,

Easy walking around Farndale Head

but clear, path darts off to the left to reach a single track road heading north across Danby High Moor; this time the saving is about 300m/yds.

> Whether you take any of the offered shortcuts from the Margery Bradley stone is a matter of personal preference. Offering little in the way of time saving they may well be shunned in favour of staying with the road, which has the advantage of visiting Ralph Cross, and is a safer guide in poor visibility.

Follow the road, left, up a slight rise, until a broad track branches right, towards an old shooting hut, Trough House. A fine traverse of moorland now ensues, the path soon meeting Trough Gill Beck and then circling the head of Great Fryup Dale across a landscape dominated by heather, bracken and bilberry, and passing an area where coal was once mined. This enjoyable interlude across Glaisdale High Moor declines as the way meets another of the unenclosed roads cross-crossing this part of the moors, this one keeping to the high ground between Great Fryup Dale and Glaisdale.

Turn left along the road, heading north, and after about 1.5 kilometres (1 mile) go right on a broad track just before the road reaches the conspicuous trig point. The track that follows, along Glaisdale Rigg, is an ancient highway, as many standing stones with directions on them testify, and leads easily and most pleasantly down to the village, with the abundant heather (not yet the last we will see) gradually giving way to grass as height is lost. Finally reaching the village at the green, the onward route here turns right, staying with the meandering road through this strung-out village to the railway station, near Beggar's Bridge. With only short stretches of heather moorland to come, the time spent in the wilderness of the North York Moors can here be said to be at an end.

GLAISDALE

Glaisdale is a sprawling village built on a series of hillsides that in the mid-nineteenth century possessed a prosperous iron industry which helped to establish nearby Middlesbrough as a steel-producing town of considerable importance.

Arthur Mee described the nearby valley as 'a dale shut off from the world by the moors', while an earlier guide proclaimed 'There is no air more vigorating, the spot has many natural charms. It is among meandering streams and wooded vales, and around for miles are the beautiful moors.' Not surprisingly, such an isolated community, one that even today is awkward to get to, is a source of folklore and legend. Prevalent in that folklore are many tales of **hobs and goblins**, and one such used to inhabit Hart Hall Farm on the edge of the village. Usually hobs are depicted as solitary, dwarf-like creatures, often shaggy-haired and ugly, a description that so far describes the author to a T. Hobs, however, often work naked and dislike clothes to the extent that a gift of clothing would be regarded as an insult, something that would annoy them intensely causing them to become mischievous, vindictive or dangerous. Adept at hiding themselves from prying eyes, they work extremely hard and quickly, seeking no reward beyond an occasional word of thanks; if I could find a tame one capable of using a word processor, I could make a fortune!

The hob at Hart Hall Farm apparently was a kindly fellow, and much loved by the inhabitants of the farm.

Most of the crosses on the moors are now without the cross-piece, being little more than a base or simple pillar. Used originally to guide travellers across the moors, they are found at strategic points (that is, medievally strategic), and serve these days to indicate the line of ancient tracks and cross-moor routes. Anyone interested in pursuing a study of these crosses will find Stanhope White's book *Standing Stones and Earth works of the North York Moors* (1987), of particular interest.

Once, when a hay wagon wheel became jammed between stones, with bad weather threatening, it became vital that the hay was brought in from the fields without delay. But all efforts to release the wheel failed, and the tired farm hands went to bed that night facing a harder than usual day's work in the morning. But, during the night, the hob got to work, using his great strength to release the wheel, and drawing the fully laden wagon into the farmyard. When dawn came, the farm hands found the hay not only down from the fields and stacked, but the wagon prepared for the next day.

This sort of tale typically reflects the beliefs prevalent in these isolated communities. Always, it seems, the hobs were there when needed, helping with every chore around the farm, and always in secret. No one ever saw the hobs at work or heard them, and it would take a brave person to dismiss these accounts off hand. Whatever our modern interpretation or opinions might be, they formed a real, and no doubt psychologically supportive, element in the daily round of people destined to spend their lives in simple, hard, rural toil.

The route through Glaisdale could not be simpler; follow the road to the station. A passageway just before the terrace containing the post office leads to a quieter back road through the village, as does a narrow road opposite the Mitre Hotel. All come together again near the railway station.

Glaisdale (Beggar's Bridge) to Grosmont

Distance: 5.7 kilometres (3.5 miles)
Ascent: 25 metres (80 feet)

Strong walkers will find this last section, to Robin Hood's Bay, well within their grasp. It is, nevertheless, long, and comes hard on the heels of a long day before. Careful planning of these final days is therefore of key importance, and if some advantage can be gained from being ferried about by helpful bed and breakfast proprietors then make use of them; it would be a shame to

arrive at the spectacular end too jaded to appreciate it
(see Planning the Walk in the Handbook section).

At Glaisdale railway station the road bends right to pass beneath the railway bridge. Immediately before the bridge, a path goes right (signposted) over a footbridge spanning Glaisdale Beck to enter East Arncliff Wood. Before taking this route, however, a short diversion under the railway bridge is needed to visit Beggar's Bridge.

> **Beggar's Bridge** is, it is claimed, the handiwork of one **Tom Ferris**, a local man of modest means who fell in love with Agnes Richardson, the daughter of a wealthy farmer from Egton. The River Esk at this spot is always difficult to cross, the more so when in spate, but to see Agnes, Tom had to negotiate its watery ways. Agnes' father, however, seeing little in Tom's prospects, did his best to end the relationship, inevitably forcing the couple to meet in secret. With so much opposition it became clear that if he intended to have his bride, Tom had to make his fortune. Fortunately, he liked travelling, and left Glaisdale to join a ship at Whitby. Before long he found himself fighting the Spanish Armada, after which he (perhaps unavoidably) turned to looting Spanish galleons. Eventually, he returned, and rose to become Mayor of Hull and Warden of its Trinity House. With his future assured, Tom built his famous bridge in 1619, and married Agnes.
>
> Obviously serving a packhorse trade route across the moors, the bridge is a remarkable and pleasing structure, its sides leaning outwards to accommodate bulging side packs, or panniers. Soon the walk encounters a paved pannier-way as it enters East Arncliff Wood.

Retreat beneath the railway bridge to cross Glaisdale Beck, where the path climbs steeply for a while, leading on to an extended paved way, one of the centuries-old pannier-ways. Amid the quiet, green shelter of this natural woodland, the path seems longer than it is, concluding finally as it emerges onto a quiet road. Here turn left, down the hill to Egton Bridge.

Egton Bridge is one of Yorkshire's most beautiful villages, occupying a superb site on the River Esk, and flanked by great stands of trees and verdant loveliness. Its name comes from 'Egetune', meaning 'town of oaks', and with its neighbour, Egton, on the hillside a short distance away, was given by William the Conqueror to his blacksmith in 1070. The village is renowned for its adherence to the Roman Catholic faith, so strong that it caused it to become known as 'the village missed by the Reformation', and was the birthplace in 1596 of **Nicholas Postgate**.

Postgate, later called 'Blessed Nicholas Postgate, Martyr of the Moors', at the age of twenty-five went to be trained as a priest in France, something that was illegal in England. After his ordainment he was sent to England as a missionary, and spent the early part of his priesthood as chaplain to a number of wealthy families, his true role being concealed by his work as a gardener. Understandably, he always travelled in disguise and in secret to say Mass, give communion and visit the sick. His love of gardening prompted him to plant flowers on his travels, and he is credited with bringing the wild daffodil to the moors, calling it the Lenten Lily. Yet, in spite of the many efforts to keep his work concealed, he was finally betrayed by an exciseman at Whitby called John Reeves, who set a trap for Postgate and had him arrested while conducting a baptism at Red Barns Farm, near Ugglebarnby. Reeves received the princely sum of £20 for his work, Postgate was charged with High Treason for which he was hung, drawn and quartered on the 7th August 1679, at the age of 82.

Sadly, Postgate's last resting place is unknown, though relics of his work, and of the Postgate Society founded in his memory, can be sent at St Hedda's Catholic Church in Egton Bridge. The true significance of Nicholas Postgate's dedication to his faith can be weighed by the fact that during the first-ever visit to England by a reigning pope, in 1982, Pope John Paul II stood on Postgate's place of execution (now part of the Racecourse at York) and prayed a litany of northern saints, including Nicholas Postgate among them.

As a footnote, and having much in common with a similar story of betrayal found in the bible, John Reeves, horrified by the outcome of his treachery, committed suicide by drowning himself in a deep pool at Littlebeck, ever since known as Devil's Dump.

On reaching Egton Bridge, at a T-junction near the Horseshoe Inn, keep ahead to cross the road bridge over the Esk. Soon, turn right to a junction between the church and Egton bridge (i.e. the bridge), leaving the village by an enclosed way (signposted: 'Egton Estates – private road'). Formerly this way was a toll road, now described as a permissive path, and finally meets the valley road near a loop in the Esk, not far from Priory Farm. A footbridge (and a ford) here enable onward passage to the road, turning right, over a bridge no more than a few strides away, though both bridges cross the same river flowing in opposite directions.

Follow the road into the village, first passing under, and then over, a railway line, though in this case the former BR's Esk valley line, and the latter the privately-operated North Yorkshire Moors Railway.

The building of one of the railway lines, in 1836, exposed a rich seam of ironstone of the highest quality that ultimately yielded over 100,000 tons of ore each year before the mining ended in 1871. The ore was transported by rail to the coast at Whitby, for shipping to the Tyne, and the presence of railways still features largely in the every-day life of touristy Grosmont. Destined to pass into

In their all-conquering manner, the Romans built a road through Grosmont (pronounced grow-mont), and a fort to protect it, taking advantage of its strategic position at the confluence of two rivers, the Esk and the Murk Esk. There is scant evidence of Grosmont's ancient history, though in around 1200 Johanna Fossard, supported by the French priory of Grandimont, founded a priory here. No trace remains today, but it is known to have occupied the site of present-day Priory Farm.

oblivion, the Whitby–Pickering line, opened in 1836, as a horse-drawn tramway intended to help the development of the timber, sandstone and limestone industries found inland, was closed in 1965. However, in 1967 the North Yorkshire Moors Preservation Society was formed, and managed to purchase the line from Grosmont to Eller Beck. More bureaucratic wranglings ensued until, finally, on the 1st May 1973, the **North York Moors Railway** was formally opened by the Duchess of Kent. It is now a fascinating and absorbing diversion, enjoying great popularity.

Grosmont to Robin Hood's Bay

Distance: 23 kilometres (14.5 miles)
Ascent: 475 metres (1560 feet)

So, wherever you spent last night, this really is the final leg of the journey, one to be savoured and enjoyed, one to be embarked upon with both a sense of happiness and of sadness: happy to have achieved our personal goal, to have overcome such adversity as we might have encountered, to have triumphed, and sad that such a good thing is coming to an end. There will have been bad days, almost certainly, when spirits were low, or feet and shoulders ached, or the pub closed two minutes before you reached it. But the greater part will be of good memories, unsurpassed scenery, historic moments (in more than one sense, no doubt), good companionship (perhaps), and walking of the highest order (most certainly). Anyone who found nothing of pleasure in the crossing is either emotionally spent, or but one step away.

Leave Grosmont by climbing east (ignoring two roads going left to 'Sleights'), and continuing up Fair Head Lane.

Fair Head Lane is a tiring pull at the best of times, but is eased a little by fine retrospective views over the Esk valley. More significantly, Whitby Abbey can be seen in the distance on its clifftop site, as the final chapter of the walk draws inexorably to a close.

When the lane reaches the open moor, a track goes right to locate a line of standing stones known as the Low Bride Stones. Further on, by a sketchy path, the High Bride Stones are encountered, before the path returns to the road. Cross the road, and continue by a narrow trod through heather to the tumulus of Flat Howe on the high ground of Sleights Moor.

Blue Bank was the first surfaced road in the Whitby district, being built in 1759 to link Whitby to Saltersgate via Sleights. By 1788 it had aspired to a twice-a-week cart service, linking Whitby, Pickering and York.

> **Low Bride Stones** are something of a disappointment, lying haphazardly in a boggy depression, while **High Bride Stones** make a more determined effort to remain upright in the face of the elements.
>
> From the elevated, heather-clad vantage point of Flat Howe more of the coastline springs into view, a splendid and long-awaited moment, with Whitby seen almost in its entirety, an exciting panorama arousing a slight, but now steadily growing sensation of nearing the end. Moving south along the coast from Whitby a depression in the cliffline pinpoints our final destination, while further south still, and moving a little inland, the 'golf balls' of the **Fylingdales Early Warning Station** look silly against a backdrop that is so predominantly natural. What would prehistoric man, who long ago inhabited these wild moors, make of such a monstrosity?

From Flat Howe a path descends to meet the A169 at the top of Blue Bank, gaining access to the roadside at a stile.

Go right, up the road, for a few strides to locate a stile on the opposite side of the road, which gives onto a bridleway heading down to the ensuing moor to reach a stony track. Continue down the track to meet the narrow and twisting metalled road leading to the hamlet of Littlebeck.

> **Littlebeck** is every bit as charming a retreat as many of the villages encountered along the walk, a secluded and sheltered community unsuspected from afar, but renowned locally for the extravagant beauty of its woodland.

Press on down to the hamlet and start ascending the road leading away from it. At a second bend go right, through a gate (signposted: 'C-to-C' and 'Falling Foss'). Enter the woodland to begin a delightful, but brief interlude in the company of Little Beck. A good path leads on, negotiates a tributary stream, and leads to the unexpected sight of a spoil heap. Such an apparition, at this stage in the walk, only arouses a casual inspection, it is no more than it seems to be, and is passed using a flight of steps to reach a muddy path, slithering onwards for a while before arriving at a huge boulder on the left, known as the Hermitage.

From the Hermitage continue along the higher of two paths that follow, and when this shortly forks take the right branch to Falling Foss, a lovely waterfall in a wooded setting, always delightful, but at its best after prolonged rain. Nearby, the ruins of Midge Hall are reached by a footbridge; a stone block set in a gate pillar here bears the inscription 'Sneaton Lordship'.

Continue alongside the stream, with a larger, farm access bridge appearing on the left. Cross the access track and keep ahead to reach the stream at a ford. If the stream is in flood, or the prospect of a dunking at this late stage in the journey proves a deterrent to heroics, backtrack to the farm bridge, and locate a path on the opposite bank that will bring you to the same spot.

The path continues ahead to meet a broader forest trail, at which go right, to cross a stream by a footbridge, continuing ahead on an improving path, passing to the left a pond with bullrushes, and keeping onwards to reach the vicinity of May Beck car park.

On reaching May Beck bridge go immediately left on the road, doubling back, and following the road to, and beyond, a bend near New May Beck Farm. As the road straightens, leave it, right, on a broad public footpath (signposted), that soon deteriorates to a narrow path across Sneaton Low Moor, where the onward route is marked by occasional guideposts.

Arrival at the B1416, Ruswarp road, is at a low stile opposite a narrow plantation and Raikes Lane.

> This moment is one to check how well you are doing in terms of your estimated finishing time. If all is well, continue with the route below. But if time has become a pressing concern, a number of shortcuts are to hand, and are mentioned in the Handbook section (see Planning the Walk).

Turn right along the B1416 for about 700m/yds to a stile and gate on the left (signposted: 'C-to-C'). Now follow a narrow trod through low heather scrub across what is to be the final stretch of moorland. The path, marked by an occasional guidepost, is frequently wet, and passes through a couple of boggy depressions. This short stretch rejoices in the name of Graystone Hills, an appellation heavy with descriptive licence. With a final boggy flourish the path arrives at a gate, close by a raised tumulus on the right. For the record, the steps that take you across the gate-stile will be the last of the journey on moorland.

Keep to the field edge in the ensuing pasture to arrive at

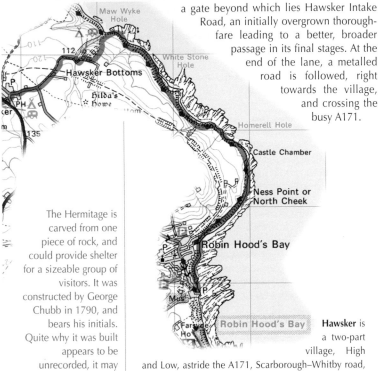

a gate beyond which lies Hawsker Intake Road, an initially overgrown thoroughfare leading to a better, broader passage in its final stages. At the end of the lane, a metalled road is followed, right towards the village, and crossing the busy A171.

The Hermitage is carved from one piece of rock, and could provide shelter for a sizeable group of visitors. It was constructed by George Chubb in 1790, and bears his initials. Quite why it was built appears to be unrecorded, it may simply have been to serve the purposes of a local eccentric, an eighteenth-century form of escapism that sees its modern counterpart in the CD player-decked brigade that wander blank-faced about our streets, or sit to all intents and purposes immutably insular on trains and buses.

Hawsker is a two-part village, High and Low, astride the A171, Scarborough–Whitby road, with the greater portion located across the road. Here roadside benches invite a moment's respite, while a telephone is handy for walkers still needing to finalise accommodation arrangements.

At Hawsker is one of Yorkshire's many legendary links with Robin Hood, and since his bay is close by, it justifies re-telling. The story is that both Robin and Little John, on a visit to Whitby, were accommodated at the abbey, where they were invited to demonstrate their archery skills. From the top of an abbey tower they each fired an arrow to the southwest, and each landed on Whitby Laithes, a stretch of ground, now a farm, near Hawsker. So impressed was the abbot with these shots that he ordered standing stones to be fixed where the arrows had landed, and to this day those places, Robin Hood's Field and Little John's Field, are still shown on maps. That the arrows would have had to carry a distance of just over two kilometres (one-and-a-quarter miles) for this to be an accurate account is the sort of puerile currency that sceptics deal in to spoil a good yarn – have we not all employed a little hyperbolic colouring at some time in our lives?

Leave the village up the road (signposted: 'Robin Hood's Bay') to the right, noting a small well on the right bearing the initials 'TC' and the date 1790. Ascend the road to a right-hand bend, and here leave it, left, for a metalled road leading to, and past, a caravan site. Another caravan site is encountered a short way further on, and here, keeping the site shop on the left, go ahead to a signposted footpath leading incongruously down through ranks of static caravans towards the North Sea.

At the bottom end of the caravan park a track runs ahead to a small filtration plant protected by fencing, to the left of which a path runs down a field alongside Oakham Beck to rejoin the Cleveland Way and meet the coastal path directly above Maw Wyke Hole, a truly

High Hawsker – village detail

breathtaking moment. Only a final scamper to Robin Hood's Bay remains, and we'll do that on all fours, if need be!

Now go right, following the coastal path, a popular, well-used and well-worn route that requires little description. Accompanying it most of the way is either a fence or a wall, sometimes both, usually on the seaward side, each field boundary crossed by stiles, as the route curves round North Cheek (Ness Point).

> Shortly after passing a Coastguard Lookout Station the broad sweep of Robin Hood's Bay finally comes into view, a tremendous, uplifting moment, as you gaze across the bay to South Cheek (Old Peak) and Ravenscar, where the Lyke Wake Walk, our sometime companion, meets its end.

Eventually, at a kissing gate go left along a path enclosed by hawthorns to emerge on a grass track in front of a row of houses. This leads on to Mount Pleasant North, at the end of which turn left on the main road down into Robin Hood's Bay, ending in a final and steep descent, through the charming cottages and shops of the old part of the village, more correctly known as Baytown, to reach the seashore.

That's it. Well done. You've finished; you can stop now…unless, of course, you dipped your boot in the sea at St Bees, or carried that pebble all the way across, in which case the necessary ceremonies must be observed.

Good organisation will see to it that champagne awaits the end of the journey: our celebrations, far out into the bay, caused a few wry smiles and looks of puzzlement. But few of the visitors you will meet at Robin Hood's Bay will have much understanding of your achievement: success, in the final analysis, is a very personal thing. Few people will know of your success, and most of those will think you are mad. But no one can take from you the knowledge that you walked across northern England, **COAST TO COAST**!

Walkers bound for the youth hostel or other accommodation at Boggle Hole can, at low tide, follow the beach. At high tide take a cliff path at the end of the main street.

ROBIN HOOD'S BAY

Legend has it that Robin Hood found a quiet bay on the edge of the northern moors and decided on this as an ideal retreat from danger. Here, under the name of Simon Wise, he returned time and time again, keeping a small fleet of fishing boats, in which he used to put to sea whenever danger threatened.

The village that bears his name was once a fishing community, with not a little emphasis on smuggling, though it has now caught the imagination of tourists, and is a popular holiday and weekend resort. Its houses and shops perch precariously at or above the water's edge, in imminent danger of collapse or flooding, many of its red roofed houses so small and narrow that they have a 'coffin window' above the door designed to enable coffins to be removed.

At high tide the sea runs into the village street, and comes in alarmingly quickly. At low tide the Scars, a layer of harder rock underlying the soft boulder clay, run far out to sea, and are full of fascinating rock pools over which to gaze before returning to the prosaic ways of every-day life.

Robin Hood's Bay

THE COAST TO COAST WALK
EAST TO WEST

In the following east to west route description additional information on sites and scenes of particular interest and on notes of historical, archaeological, sociological and other significance have been omitted. At the point in the text where they would occur a cross-reference is made to the parallel sections in the west to east description, either as a page number (21), or with a word or two of explanation (Mount Grace Priory, 144).

SECTION 5
THE NORTH YORK MOORS

ROBIN HOOD'S BAY TO GROSMONT

Distance: 23 kilometres (14.5 miles)
Ascent: 505 metres (1655 feet)

The first part of the walk in this direction seems to possess rather more uphill than the start from St Bees, but that soon eases as the exquisite scenery of the coastal path flings itself at your feet. To begin, and end, a walk in this coastal fashion is magnificent; at one end it fires the imagination, stirs the soul, at the other it serves as a compelling magnet, and offers no false reward – St Bees Head is superb, so let's get going! But not in too much haste. There are a few pretty bits in between, you know.

Climb away from the seashore at Robin Hood's Bay (169), steeply ascending through the old part of the

The North Sea near Robin Hood's Bay

village (correctly known as Baytown) to reach the main road, here continuing ahead to turn right at the Grosvenor Hotel into Mount Pleasant North (signposted: 'Cleveland Way'). At another signpost soon encountered go ahead through a gate onto a grass track in front of a row of houses quickly leading to a path enclosed by hawthorns that finally debouches, at a kissing gate, into clifftop pastures. Now follow the coastal path, the Cleveland Way, right, along the edge of numerous pastures and as far as Maw Wyke Hole, where the Coast to Coast leaves the Way for a while and assumes a westward direction by ascending left (signposted: 'Hawsker') alongside Oakham Beck to reach and pass directly through a caravan site.

At the top end of the caravan site go right to pass the site shop and then follow the road out, through its various twists and turns, to reach a bend in the B1447 not far from the village of Hawsker (166). On descending into the village go left at the first junction (near a telephone box), and then immediately right (signposted: 'Sneatonthorpe') to cross the A171. Continue ahead for about one kilometre (half a mile) until, shortly after a single rise, the route goes left along a broad track, Hawsker Intake Road, later degenerating to a narrower, overgrown path.

At the end of the path, cross a stile and follow a field boundary on the left, ahead, to another stile, beyond which lies the moorland expanse of Graystone Hills. Press on ahead, with the way through heather and the occasional boggy patch waymarked by tall posts from time to time. Eventually, the path reaches the B1416 at a stile. Go right along the road for about 700m/yds to a step stile on the left, opposite a narrow plantation and Raikes Lane. Cross the stile and head slightly left on an indistinct trod over Sneaton Low Moor, finally to reach a minor access road serving New May Beck Farm.

Turn left along the road and gradually descend to a bridge near May Beck car park. Just before the bridge, go right, along a forest trail, soon passing, on the right, a pond with bulrushes, and shortly reaching a footbridge. Cross the bridge and gain a broader trail, quickly leaving it, left, on a grassy path leading to a ford (avoided by keeping along the true right bank to a farm access bridge), and continuing ahead to the ruins of Midge Hall. At Midge Hall cross a nearby footbridge and ascend a short distance for a delightful view of Falling Foss. Continue climbing easily to reach a higher path going left to a shelter carved from rock, the Hermitage (166).

From the Hermitage press on, slightly left and down, to follow a forest path, muddy in places, finally to emerge on to a metalled road on the edge of the hamlet of Littlebeck (163). Take the road, left, out of Littlebeck, and when, after a steepish pull, it bends sharply right to head for Sleights, leave it and continue along an enclosed stony track to reach open moorland, climbing easily to the A169 at the top of Blue Bank (163).

Go right, down the road for a few strides, to locate a stile on the left on the opposite side of the road, and use it to pursue the crossing of Sleights Moor to Flat Howe, and the metalled moorland road beyond. Either go right along the road, eventually to run into Fair Head Lane, and so descend into Grosmont, or cross the road to a narrow path curving round, and passing Low Bride Stones, before rejoining the road at the top of Fair Head Lane. Follow the lane down steeply into Grosmont (162).

GROSMONT TO GLAISDALE
(BEGGAR'S BRIDGE)

Distance: 5.7 kilometres (3.5 miles)
Ascent: 70 metres (230 feet)

Keep ahead on the road through Grosmont and cross the railway line (part of the North Yorkshire Moors Railway (161)), soon bearing right, under a BR railway line to leave the village by a pleasant lane to a bend in the nearby River Esk, not far from Priory Farm. Just after the road crosses the first part of the riverbend go left to cross the second part by a footbridge (ford nearby), and then head left, on a former toll road leading to Egton Bridge.

At Egton Bridge village (159: Nicholas Postgate, 160), go left to cross the river, and climb easily on a quiet road until a path, on the right, gives access to East Arncliff Woods through which passage is eased by use of an ancient, paved pannier-way that eventually swings round and down to reach the outskirts of Glaisdale at Glaisdale Beck. Cross the beck by a footbridge, and turn left to ascend to the station. Just after crossing the footbridge, and beyond the railway viaduct on the right, stands Beggar's bridge (159: Tom Ferris, 159), well worth a moment's diversion.

GLAISDALE (BEGGAR'S BRIDGE) TO CLAY BANK TOP

Distance: 27.25 kilometres (17 miles)
Ascent: 490 metres (1605 feet)

Follow the twisting road upwards through strung-out Glaisdale (157: Hobs, 157), until, at the top of the village, at a green, a road goes left towards Glaisdale Hall Farm. The onward route now follows the line of an ancient highway, climbing at first by a grassy path and then into low heather to cross Glaisdale Rigg, high above the valley of Glaisdale to the south. Gradually the trail broadens out, and eventually meets the metalled moorland road from Lealholm to Rosedale Abbey high on a narrow neck of land sandwiched between Glaisdale and Great Fryup Dale. Go left along the road for about 1.5 kilometres (1 mile), leaving it by a rough track heading right (southwest), and swinging around the head of Great Fryup Dale to an old shooting hut, Trough House, shortly after which another unenclosed moorland road is reached.

Between this point and the Lion Inn at the top of Blakey Ridge, the simplest line is to follow the roads, not so traumatic an experience as one might expect, since they all have good verges and (other than at weekends) little traffic. It is possible to shortcut a few obvious corners by delving into bog and heather and so save a little time, but otherwise this option has nothing to commend it.

From the road just after Trough House go left at a junction, and there turn right (this corner can be cut by a path through heather). Follow the road to another junction, passing a low moorland cross on the right (Fat Betty). This stretch of road walking is avoidable by following a line of old boundary stones, saving about 100m/yds. Continue to a further junction near a car park and not far from another moorland cross, Ralph Cross (155: Moorland Crosses, 154), which has been adopted as the symbol of the North York Moors National Park. At the junction turn left, and continue as far as the Lion Inn, passing, on the right, a large, ungainly standing stone, with the name Margery Bradley. (The stretch between Fat Betty and Margery Bradley can be linked directly by a muddy path around Rosedale Head, saving a few minutes.)

As the Lion Inn is approached (a certain waylayer of walkers on a hot day), a path rises right to an ancient raised mound, Blakey Howe, that in more recent times was used for cockfighting. At the mound, head right, following a wall and descending slightly to meet the trackbed of the Rosedale Ironstone Railway (153). At a track go right, and follow this easy route for almost 8 kilometres (5 miles) around the head of Farndale until, at a gate, the Cleveland Way, unheralded, reappears obliquely from the right. Continue ahead, and, a few hundred metres/yards after a second gate, at a place known as Bloworth Crossing, leave the trackbed, descending left, and then climbing from a boggy depression to start the ascent of Urra Moor.

The summit of Urra Moor is Round Hill, the highest point of the North York Moors, and has an ancient guide post, the Hand Stone (153) nearby. Beyond the high point the track eases onwards, gradually descending Carr Ridge, and then dropping suddenly through a narrow cleft in the rock lip before plunging down to Clay Bank Top.

CLAY BANK TOP TO INGLEBY CROSS

Distance: 18.4 kilometres (11.5 miles)
Ascent: 610 metres (2000 feet)

Clay Bank Top is more correctly known as 'Hagg's Gate', and directly opposite the point at which the path from

Carr Ridge meets the B1257 Stokesley–Helmsley road a gate gives onto a rough flight of steps and a path climbing beside a wall, with a plantation on the right, to a stile. A speedy alternative route keeps in right, along the edge of the plantation, and passing round Hasty Bank and Cold Moor to rejoin the main route below the ascent of Cringle Moor.

The main line tackles the steep pull to Hasty Bank, then following the escarpment edge around to arrive shortly at the Wainstones, a tumble of boulders and rock walls, through which a number of paths thread away, descending easily through two lateral walls to a gate at Garfit Gap. More ascent leads onto Cold Moor, followed by an easy descent to a gate, round by a wall, to reach a gate at a wall corner where the alternative low level route comes in from the right.

Go left here along a Land Rover track to the broad col below Cringle Moor, and start climbing through more boulders, stones and mining debris (Jet, 148: Alum, 149) to reach the escarpment path around Cringle Moor, the highest point of which is Drake Howe, finally to arrive at a view indicator and stone seat at Cringle End (150). A good, broad path now descends with a wall on the right, to a gate, then following a green path to pass close by Lord Stones Café (Toilets and Information Centre) hidden among trees, before continuing to a minor metalled road at a gate and stile ('Three Lords' Stone', 150).

Go right, along the road for a short distance and then bear left onto a broad shaly track leading to debris from former alum quarries. At a signpost, near a small plantation, head right, ascending through quarrying debris to the rim of Carlton Moor, the summit of which is marked by a trig and boundary post (Ladybirds, 149). A good path continues from the trig, and soon encounters a long, barren strip of ground and some sad looking buildings on the left. This is the runway and headquarters of a glider station, between which and the edge of Carlton Moor the path continues ahead. An undulating passage ensues as the path presses on to Live Moor before finally dropping from the western edge of the Cleveland Hills to head for the Vale of Mowbray.

Once the top of Live Moor is passed, a broad path continues gently downwards, with good views ahead of the awaiting vale and the distant frieze of Swaledale fells. The path leads directly into a plantation at a stile leading to a steeply descending flight of wooden steps. At the bottom cross another stile and go left, following the forest boundary for a while, and shortly, at a stile, gaining an enclosed path leading to Huthwaite Green at the head of Scugdale.

On reaching the road, near a telephone box, continue ahead down a narrow lane leading to Hollin Hill Farm. The farm is passed and then Scugdale Beck, just beyond which a track branches right from the metalled roadway to a footbridge (and ford) over Piper Beck. At a gate continue ahead, up a field, to gain Clain Wood at a stile, there following a hardcore path around its perimeter to an access road. Turn left here, and then almost immediately right, to begin a steady pull into a further section of Clain Wood, meeting a broad forest trail just after a gate. A small clearing in the forest on the right gives a splendid view over Swainby. At a sign-post ('Cleveland Way'), leave the forest trail to begin a steady descent on a woodland path to reach Scarth Nick (147), at a stile.

Go left along the metalled road through Scarth Nick, crossing a cattle grid, and, in a few paces, take a signposted path on the right, climbing by flights of steps to join a broad track heading out across Scarth Wood Moor (146). The track across the moor ends at a gate, where it then follows a path sandwiched between a wall on the left and the escarpment on the right. The summit of Beacon Hill is soon reached, and marks the original starting point of the Lyke Wake Walk (147), a good stretch of which has been followed for some time. Soon the incongruous ironmongery of Beacon Hill's Radio Station looms into view, with just enough room to allow the path to squeeze by before it starts descending through South Wood.

At the southern limit of the wood, the path approaches a gate. Walkers wishing to continue to Osmotherly (145) should continue ahead through a gate, following the route briefly described on page 145. Walkers heading for Ingleby Cross should here double back, right, to continue on a broad forest trail, leaving behind the Cleveland Way, which, like the Lyke Wake Walk, has been our companion for some time.

The forest trail continues pleasantly and uneventfully, branching left at a junction, and soon passing the entrance to Park House (North York Moors Adventure Centre), by means of which, and a continuing path, a diversion can be followed to visit Mount Grace Priory (144). If not making any diversions, continue past the track to Park House, gradually descending until, as a distinct branch goes left to a gate, the forest can be left to cross a field to a gate giving onto a quiet backroad at the rear of Arncliff Hall. Follow the road, right, curving round past the hall and the nearby church, to run out to meet the A172. Cross the road, and continue ahead to reach Ingleby Cross.

SECTION 4 – THE VALE OF MOWBRAY

INGLEBY CROSS TO DANBY WISKE

Distance: 14 kilometres (8.75 miles)
Ascent: 15 metres (50 feet)

Continue up the lane, away from Ingleby Cross, and at the top, at Ingleby Arncliffe, go left and then immediately right to follow a lane out to the A19. Cross this busy dual carriageway ahead, and press on down an access lane, then following a series of left and right turns to reach the ruins of Brecken Hill Farm. Pass round the farm buildings and pursue a path, shortly descending a cornfield, to reach a footbridge over the River Wiske. Keep ahead across the ensuing field to a gate, near Sydal Lodge. Passing an open barn and the farm buildings on the left, keep ahead to follow the access track out to a minor road. Turn left along the road and then shortly right, soon keeping left again, leaving the metalled road surface for a rough track, Low Moor Lane, that continues to Harsley Grove Farm.

As the farm is approached so the condition of Low Moor Lane improves, and is followed left, away from the farm, with a fenced pasture on the right. When the fencing ends, turn right and follow the field boundary round two sides of an open meadow to a half-concealed dip on the right leading first to a sleeper bridge spanning a ditch, and, in a few strides, to a narrow, metal footbridge between stiles. Once across the footbridge ascend the cornfield ahead to a concrete stile giving pedestrian access to a crossing of a railway line. Safely across the railway go obliquely left to a hedgerow and fence leading to a gate, near Wray House. Follow the broad track away from Wray House to reach Long Lane, a minor Roman road.

Head right, up Long Lane, for about 200m/yds, and then turn left to approach Northfield House Farm. Keep the farm buildings on the right, passing round them on an access track, soon to reach a step-stile (waymarked), by which to gain access to a meadow. A green path heads across the meadow, passing Northfield Farm, and crossing an intermediate fence at a stile. Keep ahead across a second meadow to a stile and sleeper bridge, and then on along a margin field to an open barn and the ruins of Brompton Moor Farm. Cross a stile, near the barn, and head half-left to cross a stream by a footbridge, and then ahead for a short distance to a lateral field boundary. Through a gap, the path follows the field boundary round to the right, eventually arriving at a stile giving access to a small paddock adjoining Moor House Farm. Head diagonally left across the paddock to a gate, and then leave the farm buildings behind by taking the farm access track out to a minor road, Deighton Lane.

Turn left onto Deighton Lane, but after only a short distance leave it, right, for a green lane, flanked by hedgerows, passing White House Farm. Gradually the green lane narrows and becomes more overgrown, but leads eventually to a stile and an open meadow. A low hedgerow on the left guides you to a gate beyond which another green path leads out to meet the A167 almost opposite Oaktree Farm.

Head left, down the A167, and continue past the

Oaktree Hill garage, soon leaving the main road for a minor road, on the right, Crowfoot Lane, which meets the road into Danby Wiske at a T-junction. At the junction, turn right, and follow the road into Danby Wiske.

DANBY WISKE TO BOLTON-ON-SWALE

Distance: 11 kilometres (6.9 miles)
Ascent: 55 metres (180 feet)

This linking of Danby Wiske and Bolton-on-Swale makes what it can of rarely-trodden rights-of-way across, though generally around, farm fields. If time is of the essence, it is a better to follow the alternative route along the road, detailed on page 182.

On reaching Danby Wiske, go left at the White Swan Inn, down Mounstrall Lane, for about 600m/yds, leaving this minor road by a gate on the right, and follow a field margin to another gate giving access to an overgrown and enclosed way that leads us on for a while. After about 1.5 kilometres (1 mile) mostly of field boundaries, a quick left and then right (where a couple of footpaths converge) leads to a broad access track serving High Brockholme Farm and runs out to meet the road from Streetlam. Turn right on reaching this road for 400m/yds, and then left, opposite Middle Brockholme Farm, to follow a waymarked path across fields to Moor House Farm. Keep to the left of the farm buildings, negotiating some rather boggy conditions, and, at a gate near the farm house, turning left on a broad access track serving both Moor House and Red House Farms. Follow the track out to meet the B6271 at a bend. Without actually reaching the road, take a signposted path on the right, at first following a field margin on the left, and then crossing the field, keeping ahead for a short distance, to reach another field margin (now on the right) at a corner. Keep with the hedgerow to run on past Stanhowe Cottages, and, always keeping to field margins, so arrive at a gated access to a short enclosed track, once more running out, past a couple of houses, to the B6271.

Now follow the B-road, right, for about one kilometre (0.6 miles) until, just before Ellerton Bridge, a signposted path on the right heads through two gates and along field boundaries to reach the row of houses at Ellerton Hill, here turning left.

Shortly after leaving the houses at Ellerton Hill the road is left at a stile on the right, to cross pastures on a green path, more or less always ahead and in the company of Bolton Beck, until the outskirts of Bolton-on-Swale are reached. On reaching the metalled road at Bolton-on-Swale by a stile in a field corner, go left to reach St Mary's Church (132: Henry Jenkins, 132).

Variant: *This variant route between Danby Wiske and Bolton-on-Swale, with one short stretch as far as Streetlam along field boundaries, is entirely road walking, and though the roads are quiet, it has no merit other than speed.*

DANBY WISKE TO BOLTON-ON-SWALE

Distance: 10 kilometres (6.25 miles)
Ascent: 55 metres (180 feet)

Keep ahead through Danby Wiske and either follow the road all the way to Streetlam, or leave it after about one kilometre (0.6 mile) by a farm access track on the left, leading to Middle Farm. Long before reaching the farm, follow a signposted path, right, along a field boundary towards West Farm, then continuing ahead along more field boundaries to rejoin the metalled roadway at Streetlam.

At Streetlam, keep ahead at a road junction following a minor road all the way to Ellerton Hill, with only a slight variation, left then immediately right, near Hodber Hill Plantation, to arouse one from a state of quiet meditation.

Rejoin the main route as it meets the minor road near the houses at Ellerton Hill.

BOLTON-ON-SWALE TO RICHMOND

Distance: 11.2 kilometres (7 miles)
Ascent: 100 metres (330 feet)

Opposite St Mary's Church take the side road leading up to the B6271, near the village pump, and head along the B-road for a short distance to a track on the left, Flat Lane, which should now be followed through its various twists and turns, until it rejoins the B6271. Turn left, shortly, just after some gravel works, to reach a signposted path dropping left through a hedgerow to approach the banks of the River Swale, the first close encounter with the river we are now to follow virtually to its source.

Continue in company with the river as far as Catterick Bridge (130), where the walk meets the A6136 (the old A1). Go left across the bridge, and cross the road near the racecourse, and opposite the Bridge House Hotel (130). Leave the road, by going right through a gate (of sorts) and across an overflow car park, to follow an initially indistinct path to pass under a defunct railway line, then keeping ahead to pass under the A1.

Once beyond the A1, take a path ascending obliquely left to Thornborough Farm, and, keeping the farm buildings on the left, continue ahead to reach open pastures. A path skirts the fields for some distance, finally reaching the access road to St Giles Farm near a cattle grid. Head towards the farm, but leave the access road at a signposted stile on the right, moving slightly

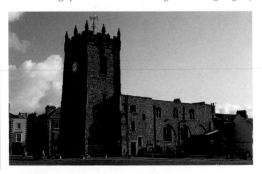

Parish Church, Richmond

away from the farm buildings in an improving path (St Giles Hospital, 130). The path leads on above the Swale to a couple of gates, at the top edge of Colburn Beck Wood, shortly going left at a stile and along a field boundary to meet a farm access. Turn right here, and keep head to enter a farmyard, there turning right, and following a track out to the edge of Colburn village.

On emerging from the farmyard, go ahead towards the village, passing a pub on the left, crossing a bridge, and then ahead onto a quiet driveway leading into woodland and alongside a small stream. Follow the accompanying path as it rises from the woodland to cross a field, and then another. At a stile, cross the next field to a slight brow, beyond which the path continues by means of an overgrown path to the ruins of Hagg Farm. The path beyond Hagg Farm re-enters woodland, passing through it on a muddy path that finally emerges into daylight at a stile, and not far from sewage works. Follow the boundary fence of the sewage works to meet its access road, and then press on to meet the main road, the A6136, at a bend. Turn right along the road for about 700m/yds, leaving it at a signposted road on the left, continuing in front of a row of houses (Priory Villas) to pass between two scruffy barns. In the field that follows take a green path ascending slightly to the left until more woodland is entered, running out eventually on the edge of a playing field beneath the ramparts of Richmond Castle. Follow the playing field boundary ahead to reach the road into Richmond and here turn right, cross Richmond Bridge (128), and ascend ahead to the town centre via Bridge Street and New Street, finally to arrive at the Market Place.

SECTION 3 – INTO THE DALES

RICHMOND TO REETH

Distance: 16.5 kilometres (10.3 miles)
Ascent: 375 metres (1230 feet)

Cross the cobbled Market Place, leaving it down Kings

Street to reach a roundabout opposite the Tourist Information Office. Turn left along Victoria Road until, near a corner shop and post office, you can leave the town, climbing steadily along a back road, Westfields, to run on, as a broad track, past High Leases and into Whitcliffe Wood (123).

On leaving Whitcliffe Wood, the path passes beneath Whitcliffe Scar (Willance's Leap, 123), and continues towards East Applegarth Farm. A waymarked path keeps above the farm, and runs on to the vicinity of High Applegarth, Low Applegarth, and soon, the last of the farms, West Applegarth, close by the eastern edge of Applegarth Scar. Take the broad access away from West Applegarth as far as a large cairn, and here descend left to cross Clapgate Beck by a footbridge. Cross the ensuing fields to rise gradually to a metalled road leading left to the village of Marske (122).

Descend through the village, cross a stream, and at a road junction follow the road ahead, past Marske Hall, and ignoring a side road to Skelton. A stiff pull ensues. Continue up the road to a gap stile on the left, by means of which a wall may be followed to reach the gate. Press on along the wall for a while, and as Hollins Farm comes into view move right, across the field, to a stile, from there skirting the farm buildings to reach its access road (Hutton's Monument, 121).

Go out along the access road for a short distance to a gate on the left, and there head across two fields to the

Striding out towards Ellers. Hollins Farm in the middle distance

renovated cottage of Ellers. More green paths across fields lead to an access serving Nun Cote Nook Farm, which is followed, right, for a few strides, until a path climbs left across yet more fields, become increasingly cluttered with rusting and derelict farm equipment on the approach to Marrick. The onward route is always waymarked, and leads to an enclosed lane running down towards the old school. The road here swings around the school and heads towards a row of cottages, the first of which boasts an unusual sundial on its wall. Go left here to a junction, near a telephone box, and then left again, on a quiet road, keeping left at another junction to leave the village past a converted Wesleyan chapel.

Always following a wall on the left, the path presses on to the top edge of Steps Wood, where a paved way, known as the 'Nun's Causeway' or 'Nunnery Steps', leads to the bottom edge of the wood, and on by a descending path to Marrick Priory (119).

Go right along the road leading away from the priory, leaving it at a stile on the left to descend to the River Swale once more, following the course of the river as far as Grinton Bridge. Cross the road at the bridge and head diagonally right across fields on a green path, swinging round to meet the road close by Reeth Bridge. Follow the road, left, over the bridge and up into the centre of Reeth (118).

REETH TO KELD

Distance: 17 kilometres (10.5 miles)
Ascent: 625 metres (2050 feet)

Leave Reeth on the B6270 for about 250m/yds to a sign-posted track, Skelgate Lane, on the right. Follow the track upwards and round to emerge at the intake wall. Go left, above the wall, keeping ahead as far as Moorcock Cottage, where the path descends to farm buildings at Thirns. Shortly after the farm, when the path forks, take the right branch, climbing gently. A fine moorland path ensues, keeping ahead, as far as the intervening gully of Cringley Bottom. Cross the gully

Two lines link Reeth and Keld; one is a high level route trekking across the desolate mining wastelands north of the valley, and of keen interest to industrial archaeologists; the other follows the river for much of the way, a fine, low level uncomplicated affair, given here as a variant (see pages 188).

with care, and continue through heather past Surrender Smelt Mill to Surrender Bridge.

Keeping on the north side of Old Gang Beck a good track continues far into a region of industrial dereliction, some of it being restored, to a gate, near in-flowing Flincher Gill. Turn left, across a bridge spanning the gill, and press on, rising steadily to the highest part of this broad and barren moorland crossing. As Gunnerside Gill is approached, so the scenery becomes even more confusing. A large cairn marks the departure, left, of a good track down towards to Gunnerside Gill (110), meeting a well-trodden terraced path still some distance above the valley bottom, and in an area of considerable spoil and debris. If you miss the cairn a signpost a short way further on ('Keld') points the way down to the same terraced path. This is followed, right, for a short distance, until a steep drop can be made to the Blakethwaite Smelt Mill.

Cross the stream by a slab bridge, and start climbing by a zigzag path to reach the top of North Hush, before swinging away, and gently upwards to arrive at a broad moorland shooters' track, near a group of modest cairns. Go right, along the track, ignoring its diversion towards the summit of Rogan's Seat, continuing ahead, still on a broad track, initially boggy, descending, right, into Swinner Gill (109). Near more smelt mills cross a fine arched stone bridge, and pass beneath the cliffs of Buzzard Scar before the path swings round to, first, an old smithy, and then the ruins of Crackpot Hall (107), where the low level route arrives from the left.

The path from Crackpot Hall continues above the river, and Kisdon Gorge, gradually descending to meet the Pennine Way for a brief moment above East Gill Force. Here, by dropping to the river, the route crosses a bridge, and climbs, right, to reach the village of Keld (103).

Variant: *The variant route that follows is quite simply self-indulgent riverside rambling, escorting the River Swale. It is a far safer and wiser choice of route if the prospect looms of inclement weather.*

REETH TO KELD ALONG THE RIVER SWALE
(LOW LEVEL ROUTE)

Distance: 19 kilometres (11.9 miles)
Ascent: 210 metres (690 feet)

Rightly described as the Royal Road, the low level route to Keld is magnificent riparian walking, in springtime and early summer across meadows lush with wild flowers.

Leave Reeth on the B6270, soon leaving it, left, down Langhorne Drive. At the bottom of the road, turn right along a quiet back road that soon deteriorates into a rough, enclosed path leading down to the river. Ignore the conspicuous footbridge across the Swale a short distance ahead, but keep on the true left bank of the river, shortly to cross in-flowing (and sometimes difficult) Barney Beck at a ford. Continue to meet the road again.

After about 1.5 kilometres (1 mile) the road is left (signposted) down a path descending into Feetham Wood. Before long the path rejoins the river, following its course all the way to Isles Bridge. Go left on the bridge for a few strides, then, without crossing it, drop right, to follow a riverside path once more until flushed up on to the road for a short distance, escaping back to the river at the first opportunity. A walk along floodbanks follows, until, for the briefest moment, the path meets and immediately leaves the road, to charge across a string of meadows to enter Gunnerside near the toilets behind the King's Head Hotel.

Turning left at the King's Head Hotel, cross the bridge spanning Gunnerside Beck, to be faced with two roads ahead. Take the one on the left; it soon leads to an estate of modern stone-built houses known as Flatlands, passed by a signposted route, to reach a meadow leading out towards the River Swale once more. On approaching the Swale, the path climbs high above the river to begin a series of meadows and squeeze stiles leading to the village of Ivelet. Here, at a telephone box, turn left, and follow a metalled road to Ivelet Bridge. Leave the road here by a gate on the right,

Patterned fields, near
Gunnerside
(low level route)

before crossing the bridge, and follow the Swale on a green path through countless meadows as it swings round towards Ramps Holme Bridge. The bridge is the means of access to Muker, for walkers staying there, or at a Usha Gap campsite, but otherwise continue ahead, ignoring the bridge, to start northwards, with the Swale a little more distant now, but always on a good path, to the foot of Swinner Gill. Cross the gill, and start climbing energetically to arrive directly beneath Crackpot Hall, where the main line of the route is rejoined, and followed to Keld.

KELD TO KIRKBY STEPHEN

Distance: 17.8 kilometres (11 miles)
Ascent: 395 metres (1295 feet)

Leave Keld by climbing up the B6270, and there turning right (youth hostel nearby). Follow the road as far as its junction with the road heading right for Tan Hill, and start up this, but only as far as a bend, there leaving the road for a footpath running along Cotterby Scar, above Smithy Holme Farm, past the gorge of Oven Mouth, and on by pleasant pastures to Ravenseat.

On reaching Ravenseat, go left to cross a bridge on the access road to this isolated community. Head out along the road and, shortly after a cattle grid, turn right, climbing easily on a boggy path towards the distant valley of Whitsun Dale. The path, following a wall on

Between Keld and Kirkby Stephen an attempt has been made, notably after Ravenseat, to keep the walk on legitimate rights-of-way or permissive paths, and to minimise problems of erosion.

the right, gradually works its way round to Ney Gill, which needs to be crossed near a wall corner. Then go left, past some sheep dipping enclosures until the wall climbs upwards, with a new path (signposted) leading to a fence and stile, near a low shelter roofed with corrugated iron (rough shelter in an emergency). Follow the right-hand wall to a signpost, and then pursue a long line of waymark posts through Whitsun Dale, always at a distance from and above the beck, finally leaving the dale along the line of Craygill Sike, climbing steadily to rejoin an older route near a peat grough on the county and National Park boundary.

Once across the grough (not easy in wet conditions), a path continues to Nine Standards Rigg, keeping ahead, past the trig and commemorative pillar to the Nine Standards (100) themselves.

From the middle of the Nine Standards an indistinct green path departs left, at right angles, soon dropping to cross a drainage channel, beyond which a more obvious path appears. Just beyond a small cairn the path forks; go left here and descend steadily on an improving path aiming for, and leading to, a pile of stones and three standing pillars, at a site known on old maps as Faraday House. Just before Faraday House it is necessary to cross Faraday Gill (98), but there the path improves significantly, and continues downwards to meet a rough, stony track running right, parallel with a wall, and leading uneventfully down to a metalled roadhead, not

Swaledale

189

far from Fell House Farm. Follow the road, past the farm, and on round the unsightly Hartley Quarries to enter the charming village of Hartley (98) itself.

The road enters the village at a sharp bend, and shortly afterwards a path (not signposted) goes left across a clapper bridge to a back lane. Follow this right for a short distance to a quiet lane on the left, leading to a gate giving access to a meadow, across which a path leads on to the River Eden (97), soon crossed at Frank's Bridge.

Over the bridge, continue ahead and then right, up Stoneshot to enter Kirkby Stephen (94) at the Market Place.

SECTION 2 – LIMESTONE COUNTRY

KIRKBY STEPHEN TO SHAP

Distance: 31.7 kilometres (19.8 miles)
Ascent: 580 metres (1900 feet)

A good part of the countryside between Kirkby Stephen and Shap has considerable archaeological and pre-history significance; it is, too, an important breeding location for birds, and these two factors have combined to engender a degree of sensitivity to disturbance caused by walkers. Over some stretches, therefore, the route has been waymarked. Where this occurs follow the →

Leave the Market Place in Kirkby Stephen by a small alleyway adjoining the Pennine Hotel, or by a similar passageway near the Black Bull Hotel. Both lead to a quieter back road. Turn left here and follow the back road past West Garth Avenue and into a narrow passage flanked by garages and a drystone wall. Gradually the road deteriorates, ceases to have a metalled surface and becomes a farm access leading to Greenriggs Farm (Croglam Castle, 92).

Enter the farmyard and turn right around the end of buildings, continuing to a waymark pointing the way, left, between the abutments of a double railway underpass. Keep ahead and shortly pass through a wall by a gate, then following a left-hand boundary of the ensuing field along a drystone wall with a group of barns just to the right. Continue to a small gate and squeeze stile. In the field that follows head directly away, climbing easily on a green path and soon following a line of waymarks, across a fence and on to a wall. A green path leads on across the next field to an underpass beneath the Settle–Carlisle railway line (92). Pass through the underpass and continue ahead on an indistinct green path aiming for a wall ahead, to the right of which there is a barn. Just after the barn, turn right, passing a solitary ash tree, and continuing easily across pastureland to a gap-stile in a drystone wall, beyond which a metalled roadway is reached. Go left along the road to a junction, and then right, following another metalled roadway, this time with a central grassy strip.

At a gate and stile on the left (signposted: 'Coast to Coast: Public Bridleway – Brownber') follow a broad farm track, keeping a drystone wall on the right. Climb easily to a high point overlooking Scandal Beck, where the wall breaks away to the right. Keep ahead here on a narrow path which becomes broader and heads for an elongated enclosure. By continuing ahead, the path gradually starts its descent to Smardale Bridge (90: Severals Settlement, 90: Pillow Mounds, 91).

Cross the bridge and swing round and upwards to the right to follow a fenceline leading to a bridge over a disused railway. Once over the bridge, ignore a prominent track ascending ahead, but keep right to a derelict railway building. There ascend left along a drystone wall, keeping above the Severals Settlement to reach a gap-stile and waymark at the top of the enclosure.

Cross the wall and continue left to a cluster of sheepfolds, there passing through a gate to begin a long and easy traverse above Bents Farm eventually to meet the Asby–Newbiggin road near a reservoir.

On reaching the unenclosed road, turn northwards, following the road, a delightful, undulating affair that passes a group of farm buildings at Mazon Wath and continues towards the limestone escarpment ahead. When it meets another road (685091), turn left (south-west), and follow the road for about 500m/yds until you can take to an indistinct footpath across untracked heather moorland, passing north of a small pond (often dried up), Spear Pots. (NOTE: There is no right-of-way across the unenclosed ground near the road junction.) Keep on to a waymarked gap-stile in a wall. Beyond the

← waymarking closely, and avoid walking over too wide an expanse of moorland; by so doing this sensitive area will be safeguarded for future walkers.

wall the path improves, and runs out to a tall fingerpost waymark at a meeting of rights-of-way. Go ahead here, following a good track to the end of an enclosed farm access leading first to Stony Head Farm, and then to Sunbiggin Farm, now on a metalled road surface. The road here is very narrow and used by farm vehicles and for herding sheep and cattle. Take care not to cause inconvenience, or to put yourself at risk.

Follow the road as far as Acres Farm, and leave it, right, to cross a number of large pastures and north–south enclosures to reach Knott Lane at a gate and stile.

A choice of routes is now available; which you choose will depend on whether you wish to visit Orton (86: George Whitehead, 86). If you are making for Orton, simply turn left down Knott Lane (Gamelands Stone Circle, 87) until the main road through Raisbeck and into Orton is reached, and there turn right for the village.

Alternatively, cross Knott Lane, and enter an adjoining field at a gate. Keep around the right-hand field boundary, following an uncultivated margin that leads to another metalled road near Scarside Farm. Go right here, following the road past Friar Biggins Farm, and on to Scar Side Farm, shortly after which turn right along the farm access to Broadfell Farm. Just before the farm buildings are reached, go right, along a wallside to a gate near woodland. Beyond the gate climb on a green track, past a lime kiln, to a gate just below the road across Orton Scar.

Walkers who took the opportunity to visit the charming village of Orton, will find a delightful bridleway leaves the top end of the village, rejoining the minor variant route near Broadfell Farm.

Climb up to the road, and continue ahead, across a cattle grid, to a road junction.

Either go down the road to the left (Crosby Ravensworth road), or keep ahead on a permissive path, following a shallow way, swinging round to meet the road near a wall corner.

Go right, down the Crosby Ravensworth road for a short distance, leaving it, left, for a stile leading west on to a waymarked route across the headwaters of Lyvennet

Beck, and passing en route a pile of stones climbing to be Robin Hood's Grave (84). A drystone wall remains our companion until the walk crosses Lyvennet Beck, beyond which it climbs to a group of large erratic boulders (83) on the edge of an expanse of limestone pavement, continues to be a permissive path, and is waymarked, leading on to one of many tumuli on these moors.

Aim now for the corner of a coniferous plantation, and there swing half-right, past a derelict sheepfold ('bield'), and continuing on a broad green path to a barn on the edge of a walled enclosure, that delights in the name of Potrigg. Here a much-improved path appears, and leads easily to the outskirts of Oddendale (82). Without entering the village, keep left, soon to branch left along a quarry track leading to the Hardendale Quarry. The quarry road is crossed by means of stiles, and a path then rises to a limestone lip, moving left alongside a wall, through a gate, and then swinging round to the right to head for a solitary farmhouse, The Nab.

Cross the road to nearby Hardendale (81) and, keeping The Nab Farm on the right, ascend to a gate in a wall corner. Keep ahead across two temporary fences and then bear right, descending towards the now prominent M6 motorway. The path parallels the motorway for a short distance, before arriving at a footbridge, by means of which the motorway is crossed.

On the other side, go right, across fields, to a narrow enclosed track, dipping left to pass a barn and arrive alongside the main north–south railway line. Cross the line by a bridge, and follow the path out to arrive on the A6 via Moss Grove, directly opposite the King's Arms Hotel, where turn right to the centre of Shap village (77).

SECTION 1 – ACROSS LAKELAND

SHAP TO PATTERDALE (GRISEDALE BRIDGE)

Distance: 24 kilometres (15 miles)
Ascent: 870 metres (2655 feet)

In the main text (see pages 74–76) two variant lines are

The final section of the journey roams across some of the finest landscape in Lakeland, a fine and fitting conclusion to the east–west walk. Anyone who has been struggling for the last day or so, might well consider having a day's rest in Shap before tackling what follows. The last few days to St Bees are not the most undemanding, and there seems little point arriving there totally exhausted and in no fit state to appreciate your achievement.

given between Patterdale and Shap; they are not repeated here, but by marking them on the map beforehand they become fairly simple to follow. Both, however, are quite energetic, and demand a good standard of fitness, especially in poor weather.

Head north along the A6 as far as the side road for Bampton Grange, following this to the bend at 555154, and there take the access road to Shap Abbey (72). Cross Abbey Bridge, and by a gate gain a path above the River Lowther, soon ascending obliquely up a field to a wall corner. Go left alongside the wall, crossing an ancient dyke before reaching a stile, beyond which a short boggy passage leads to a metalled road surface. Turn right and descend to a sharp bend, here leaving the road for a farm track on the right to a stile, giving access to an enclosure near a group of barns. Pass through the enclosure, leaving it at another stile, and then head directly away across a field to a wooded dell, dropping steeply to delectably-set Parish Crag Bridge. Cross the bridge and bear right, following a field boundary, and keeping Goodcroft Farm up to the left. Use the farm access out to reach Rosgill Bridge.

At the road bend near Rosgill Bridge go left at a stile, to rise across open moorland to a minor road. Go ahead, following an access track to Rawhead Farm, keeping the buildings on the right. A stile gives onto an open pasture; keep ahead across lateral field boundaries to a distant group of barns, High Park. Here follow a fence on the left down to a stile, crossing the fence and pursuing the course of Haweswater Beck, past attractive Thornthwaite Force to arrive at Naddle Bridge. Cross the road at Naddle Bridge to enter a wooded glade, at the other side of which the road into Burnbanks is reached. Go left to the village, originally constructed for workmen extending Haweswater (67) into a full-scale reservoir.

Just as the first cottages at Burnbanks are met, a road goes up to the right, and this should be followed. Later it climbs though trees, and comes out above the intake then to follow a long and beautiful course above the reservoir as far as the foot of the ridge rising to Kidsty Pike, and reached just after in-flowing Randale Beck.

The ascent to Kidsty Pike is quite tiring, but the view from the top is inspiring, as the path continues to meet the ancient Roman High Street, on the narrow neck of ground known as Straits of Riggindale.

Turn right here, and follow a path round to the minor summit, The Knott, avoiding its summit, other than by a diversion, and keeping on the path as it swings round beneath it. The path passes through a collapsed wall, and shortly abandons the direct descent to Hayeswater and Hartsop village, for a descending path heading right for Satura Crag and Angle Tarn. Beyond the tarn, the path scampers around Angletarn Pikes before threading an enjoyable way down to Boredale Hause, beneath the great mound of Place Fell.

Go left at the hause to overlook Patterdale, and then strike off and down to the right to an intake gate there going either left on a track to Patterdale village (58), or right through another gate, arriving near the valley bottom at Side Farm, and from there following an easy track out to the main valley road adjoining the George Starkey Memorial Hut.

PATTERDALE (GRISEDALE BRIDGE) TO GRASMERE (GOODY BRIDGE)

Distance: 11.1 kilometres (7 miles)
Ascent: 445 metres (1460 feet)

Leave Patterdale heading for Glenridding, and pass the church. At the next bend, leave the main road and go left on a minor road climbing to the valley of Grisedale. As the gradient eases a track leads through a gate and continues in a straightforward manner, and without cause for confusion, all the way to Grisedale Tarn (53).

Keep left of the tarn, crossing its outflow, and heading up to the obvious col on the left of Grisedale Hause. Cross the col, and on the ensuing descent, as the path forks, either go right, following Little Tongue Gill, or left, crossing a stream near some attractive falls,

Once more there are variant routes between these two communities. One takes the impressively rugged ascent of Helvellyn by Striding Edge, and definitely not, at this late stage, the place for any heroics. The →

Looking down on Patterdale from near Boredale Hause

← other tackles the minor summit, Birks, and then pulls up on to St Sunday Crag, a stiff and energetic proposition. Both these variants are considerably more demanding in an east–west direction, and should only be considered by extremely fit walkers and in good visibility. Both variants rejoin the main route at Grisedale Tarn, to which the rest of us will now saunter at a relaxed pace.

to follow Tongue Gill. Both routes join at the foot of the Great Tongue. Cross the streams near their confluence, and pass through a sheep enclosure to reach a good path descending to reach the main road at Mill Bridge.

Cross the road, and take a minor road ahead leading round to Low Mill Bridge, spanning the River Rothay, here turning left on a road later passing Thorney How Youth Hostel to arrive at Goody Bridge. Grasmere village (50) lies down the road to the left.

GRASMERE (GOODY BRIDGE) TO BORROW-DALE (ROSTHWAITE) VIA FAR EASEDALE

Distance: 11.3 kilometres (7 miles)
Ascent: 545 metres (1790 feet)

Another, signposted, variant takes the onward route over Helm Crag and Gibson Knott, a tough and tiring pull, but, following an overnight in Grasmere, at least it comes early in the day. It shares the first part of the walk with the conventional route, through Far Easedale.

Continue away from Grasmere, heading into Far

Easedale, a proposition far less confusing on the ground than it appears on the map. With the onward route never in doubt. Towards the end it climbs rather energetically to reach a grassy col at Far Easedale Head, beyond which lies the gulf of Wyth Burn, crossed by a cairned track, and climbing to Greenup Edge.

Greenup Edge is no place to be for long in poor visibility, and though the track across it is plainly evident, the spot is still potentially confusing. The onward path is cairned and leads to the top of Lining Crag, from where there is a spectacular view down the length of the valley that awaits. Through the valley a good path leads on, always keeping on the true right bank of the streams, and finally emerging into Borrowdale (45) at the rear of hotels in the village of Rosthwaite (46), reaching the valley road just north of the village.

BORROWDALE (ROSTHWAITE) TO BLACK SAIL YOUTH HOSTEL

Distance: 8.8 kilometres (5.5 miles)
Ascent: 540 metres (1770 feet)

Cross the road and take the first turning on the right, following it round between charming cottages, and shortly before going left to locate a gate on the left. Through the gate follow a wall and then a fence across a pasture of low scrub to another gate near a group of small cottages. Go past the cottages and turn right to cross a hump-back bridge spanning the River Derwent. The gated track leads to a youth hostel, and continues delightfully to emerge on a descending track to the car park at Seatoller.

Continue across the car park to the road, turning right, through Seatoller, and just after the Lake District National Park Information Centre at Dalehead Barn, go right at a gate, at first heading away from Honister, before doubling back and following the course of an old toll road to the top of the pass.

Press on over the top of the pass (Honister Youth Hostel), and by a gate enter the grounds of the Honister

The distance between Rosthwaite and the Black Sail Youth Hostel is not great, but there is the ascent to the top of Honister Pass to contend with first. Beyond Honister, however, a demanding variant crosses to Haystacks and on across the High Stile range to far off Great Borne (only for mega-fitties, this). Even so, careful thought needs to be given at this →

← stage to plan the final few days, ideally to arrive at St Bees as the sun is setting, or in time to catch a train home. But, be warned: Dent Fell is quite a sting in the tail of the Coast to Coast Walk, and its modest proportions should not be underestimated.

Slate Quarry (43). Continue beyond the buildings and in a short distance follow a path (signposted: 'Great Gable' and 'Dubs'). Climb steeply to gain the line of an old tramway used by the quarry and follow this until, as the gradient eases, you encounter an obvious path going left. Head along this, climbing gently, until at a large cairn another track branches right (Moses' Trod, 38). Take the right branch, and start gradually descending to the top of Loft Beck, a steep and friable gully (also a heat trap), that speeds you down to the head of Ennerdale, not far distant from the Black Sail Youth Hostel.

BLACK SAIL YOUTH HOSTEL TO ENNERDALE BRIDGE

Distance: 14.1 kilometres (8.8 miles)
Ascent: 40 metres (130 feet)

Easy walking now: time to relax, think back, think ahead, make more plans for next year, not to mention the joys of getting back to work!

Beyond Black Sail Youth Hostel the track forks: one branch scampers up to Scarth Gap, with the possibility, for strong walkers, of tackling the High Stile ridge. The other branch, heads off through a gate into Ennerdale Forest, following the forest trail to and beyond the youth hostel at High Gillerthwaite.

A short distance after the youth hostel a path goes left across a stream, and follows a delightful path around the southern shore of Ennerdale Water (34), grappling with Angler's Crag, and finally arriving at Crag Farm, near which the track (signposted) heads right for the outflow from the lake.

The same point may be reached rather more leisurely, by staying on the main forest trail, and keeping round the north shore of the lake.

When the two routes combine, near a forest car park, keep ahead and follow the road out, left, right, left, to Ennerdale Bridge (32).

ENNERDALE BRIDGE TO CLEATOR

Distance: 8.5 kilometres (5.3 miles)
Ascent: 380 metres (1245 feet)

Leave the village, heading west, and at a junction go left up a fell road for about 1.5 kilometres (1 mile) to a track on the right. Follow the track, but soon leave it, to enter a sheltered valley on the left, through which glows the delectable Nannycatch Beck: this ultimately runs into the valley of Uldale, a quiet and much unsuspected corner of Lakeland. Follow the obvious path to a gate and stile beneath Flat Fell (Nannycatch Gate). Turn left here, following the path for a short distance until, on the far side of Raven Crag, a horrendously steep path rockets upwards on the right to reach a stile leading into forest. Go left on a forest trail, and shortly branch right, climbing up through the forest, to emerge not far from the top of Dent Fell (30).

[In recent times there have been some problems beyond Nannycatch Gate, with the route along Nanny-catch Beck, which is not a right-of-way. If this persists, simply keep on along the road until you can branch right onto an access track to Sillathwaite Farm, and then west to Nannycatch Gate, rejoining the route there.]

From Ennerdale Bridge to St Bees is a distance of 22.1 kilometres (13.8 miles), well within the capabilities of anyone who has travelled this far. Even so, whether a last overnight halt at Cleator is justified depends largely on the time and the condition in which you wish to finish at St Bees.

Ennerdale

Continue ahead, across Dent's two tops, and down the other side, following waymarked paths to reach a metalled road near Black How Farm. A track, diagonally opposite, leads round the farm buildings and on to a track leading to Blackhow Bridge, spanning the river Ehen. Cross the bridge and go ahead until you can turn left up Kiln Brow to reach the main street of Cleator (28). Turn left for a short distance and then, opposite a public house, take the road on the right.

CLEATOR TO ST BEES

Distance: 13.6 kilometres (8.5 miles)
Ascent: 225 metres (740 feet)

Follow the road as far as the cricket ground, and go round it, passing through a succession of gates and pastures, and crossing the trackbed of a former railway in the process, finally to emerge on another road. Turn right, and walk down to the village of Moor Row (28). Near the post office, turn left and follow the road out of Moor Row, across the A595, and along an enclosed track passing beneath a disused railway. A path continues ahead to a stile, and swings left around the edge of woodland to a stile adjoining a gate. Now follow a field boundary, right, to a stile in a corner, near Stanley Pond. Cross the ensuing field, diagonally left, to reach a railway underpass. On the other side, climb the field ahead to reach a track leading to Bell House Farm, and on to the B5345.

Cross the road, and follow an access track round to Desmesne Farm, there to turn left to pursue a delightful lane running out to Lane Head. Keep ahead, following the road round to Sandwith. At the southern edge of the village, turn right on a narrow, enclosed road, until it branches right to head for a cliff edge quarry where Whitehaven springs dramatically into view.

Keep left on reaching the quarry, and follow an obvious path around two component parts of St Bees Head, North and South Head. These are separated, most attractively so, by Fleswick Bay (25), a short incursion into the cliffs, preceded by a coastguard lookout station and St Bees Lighthouse. The path runs on in extravagantly delightful fashion, finally descending dramatically to the seashore at St Bees (21).

Once across Rottington Beck you may consider that you have completed the walk across northern England, **COAST TO COAST**.

Congratulations: Well done!

Let's hope you still have enough energy and determination left to celebrate this considerable achievement in fitting style, and that when it has all sunk in, probably some weeks hence, you will consider it to have been one of the finer moments of your life.

Looking down on Fleswick Bay from South Head, St Bees

BIBLIOGRAPHY

A Coast to Coast Walk, A Wainwright (Westmorland Gazette, 1973)

The Coast to Coast Walk, Paul Hannon (Hillside Publications, 1992)

Companion into Lakeland, Maxwell Fraser (Methuen, 3rd edn 1943)

Cumbrian Discovery, Molly Lefebure (Victor Gollancz, 1977)

The English Lake District, Molly Lefebure (B T Batsford, 1964)

The English Lakes, Frank Singleton (B T Batsford, 1954)

Geology Explained in the Lake District, Robert Prosser (David and Charles, 1977)

Geology Explained in the Yorkshire Dales and on the Yorkshire Coast, Derek Brumhead (David and Charles, 1979)

Guide to the English Lake District, M J B Baddeley (Ward, Lock and Co.)

A History of Lead Mining in the Pennines, Arthur Raistrick and Bernard Jennings (Longmans, Green & Co. Ltd, 1965)

Illustrated Lakeland Journals, Dorothy Wordsworth (Collins, 1987)

The Lake Counties: Cumberland and Westmorland, Arthur Mee (Hodder and Stoughton, 1937)

The Lake Mountains: Vols 1 and 2, Terry Marsh (Hodder and Stoughton, 1987)

The North York Moors, Nicholas Rhea (Robert Hale, 1985)

North York Moors National Park, National Park Guide No. 4, Arthur Raistrick (ed.) (HMSO, 1966)

Portrait of Cumbria, J D Marshall (Robert Hale, 1981)

Portrait of Yorkshire, Harry J Scott (Robert Hale, 1965)

Rambles in the Lake Country, Edwin Waugh (John Heywood, London, c1898)

Walking in the Lake District, H H Symonds (W & R Chambers, Edinburgh, 1947)

Walking through Eden, Neil Hanson (Pavilion Books Ltd, 1990)

The Yorkshire Pennines of the North West, W Riley (Herbert Jenkins Ltd, London, 1934)

APPENDIX 1: ACCOMMODATION GUIDE

This Accommodation Guide was originally compiled in August 1992, and updated in January 1997 and March 2002. Walkers with information to add to the guide, or comments about any of the accommodation serviced mentioned, should contact the author through the publisher. Such comments would be much appreciated and, where appropriate, treated in confidence.

The list of accommodation is not exhaustive, and is changing all the time. There are independently-published Accommodation Guides available should this listing not provide you with the lodgings you seek. Walkers should check availability and tariffs for subsequent years directly with the proprietor.

The entries have been listed alphabetically, and grouped roughly in the order in which they will be encountered, and in the sections used in the main guide. Please ensure that, when writing, the full address is used: this incorporates the headings that have been employed to group the accommodation. For example, the full address of the first proprietor is: *Mrs Pamela Dixon, Lismore Guest House, 28 Wellington Road, WHITEHAVEN, Cumbria CA28 7HE.*

BED AND BREAKFAST ACCOMMODATION

The following is a selection of accommodation available, based on information supplied by the proprietors. No attempt has been made to classify or grade the accommodation further than that detailed in the key below.

Please note: an evening meal is not always available (and should in any case always be booked in advance). The list does not indicate those proprietors who provide evening meals; but do ask. In many cases it has been found that proprietors do not provide evening meals when there are ample facilities nearby.

Some of the accommodation listed may be a short distance off the Coast to Coast route; where this is more than a quarter of a mile, the distance has usually been given, together, where applicable, with an indication that the proprietors are willing to pick up walkers from suitable points, though this service may not always be free.In any case, at the very least, offer to pay for petrol. Quite often it will be found that proprietors are willing to pick up walkers a day's walk either side of their accommodation, making the logistics easier, and enabling walkers to have a day or so without a rucsack.

The possibility of being charged also applies to the laundry facility some establishments offer.

Section 1 – Across Lakeland

Whitehaven

Lismore Guest House, 28 Wellington Row, CA28 7HE (66028): D/L: Dogs: 4 miles – No P/U.

Sandwith

Tarn Flatt Hall, Sandwith, CA28 9UX (692162): C and B: D/L; Dogs: Non-smoking.

St Bees

Manor House Hotel, 11/12 Main Street, CA27 0DE (822425): D/L: 0.5 mile – No P/U.
Outrigg House, CA27 0AN (822348): D/L: Non-smoking: (eighteenth-century house).
Queens Hotel, CA27 0DE (822287): D/L: Dogs.
Seacote Hotel, Beach Road, CA27 0ES: (822777): H and C: D/L: Dogs.
Stonehouse Farm, CA27 0DE (822224): C: D/L: Dogs.
Tomlin Guest House, Beach Road, CA27 0EN (822284): D/L: Dogs: Non-smoking in public areas.

Cleator

Ennerdale Country House Hotel, Cleator, CA23 3DT (813907): D/L: Dogs: Non-smoking: P/U from Ennerdale.

Cleator Moor

Parkside Hotel, Parkside, Cleator Moor, CA25 5HC (811001): D/L.

KEY:	
C or B	indicate that the address also has Camping or Bunkhouse/Camping Barn facilities, but see separate entry for details
D/L	Drying/Laundry facility
Dogs	Dogs Welcome
P/U	Pick up service

Ennerdale/Ennerdale Bridge

Brookside, Ennerdale Bridge, Cleator, CA23 3AR (861470): D/L: Non-smoking.
Ennerdale Village Campsite – see entry under Campsites.
The Shepherds Arms Hotel, Ennerdale, Cleator, CA23 3AR (861249): D/L: Dogs.

BORROWDALE, NR KESWICK, TELEPHONE CODE: 017687

Rosthwaite

Nook Farm (Mrs Carole Jackson), Rosthwaite, CA12 5XB (77677): D/L: Dogs.
Royal Oak Hotel (Mr and Mrs Neil and Susan Dowie), Rosthwaite, CA12 5XB (77241): D/L: Dogs.
Scafell Hotel (Mr William M Jessop), Rosthwaite, CA12 5XB (77260): D/L.

Stonethwaite

Gillercombe (Chapel Farm Campsite), Stonethwaite Road End, Rosthwaite, CA12 5XG (77602): C (GR 257142): D/L.
Langstrath Inn, Stonethwaite, CA12 5XG (77239): D/L: Non-smoking, except in bar.
Stonethwaite Farm, Stonethwaite, CA12 5XG (77234): C: D/L.

GRASMERE, TELEPHONE CODE: 015394

Fairy Glen, Swan Lane, LA22 9RH (35620): D/L.
The Grasmere Hotel, LA22 9TA (35277): D/L: Dogs.
Lake View, LA22 9TD (35384): D/L: Dogs.
Moss Grove Hotel, LA22 9SW (35251): D/L.
Oak Bank Hotel, Broadgate, LA22 9TA (35217): D/L: Dogs.
Raise View Guest House, White Bridge, LA22 9RQ (35215): D/L: Non-smoking.
Travellers Rest Inn, LA22 9RR (35604): D/L: Dogs: Non-smoking.
Wordsworth Hotel, LA22 9SW (35592): D/L.

PATTERDALE, PENRITH, TELEPHONE CODE: 017684

Glenridding

Fairlight Guest House (Mrs Helen Beaty), Glenridding, CA11 0PD (82397): D/L: Dogs: 1 mile, P/U.
Gillside Farm, Glenridding – see under entry for Campsites.

Glenridding Hotel, Glenridding, CA11 0PB (82228): D/L: Dogs: Non-smoking in restaurant.

Inn on the Lake, Glenridding, CA11 0PA (82444): D/L: Dogs: Non-smoking: 1 mile – No P/U; No weekends.

Mosscrag Guest House (Mr and Mrs John and Pauline Lake), Glenridding, CA11 0PA (82500): D/L: Non-smoking.

Hartsop

Fellside, Hartsop, CA11 0NZ (82532): D/L: Dogs: Non-smoking in bedrooms, elsewhere by mutual consent: 0.5 mile – No P/U.

Patterdale

Glebe House, Patterdale, CA11 0NL (82339).

Home Farm, Patterdale, CA11 0PU (82370): C: D/L: Dogs.

Noran Bank Farm, Patterdale, CA11 0NR (82201): Dogs.

The Patterdale Hotel, Patterdale, CA11 0NN (82231): D/L: Dogs: ('special price for coast to coast walkers').

The White Lion Inn, Patterdale, CA11 0NW (82214): Dogs.

(BAMPTON AREA) PENRITH, CUMBRIA

Askham/Bampton. Telephone Code 01931

St Patricks Well Inn, Bampton, CA10 2RQ (713244): 2 miles – No P/U.

Bampton/Bampton Grange. Telephone Code 01931

Crown and Mitre, Bampton Grange, CA10 2QR (713225): D/L: Dogs:1 ¼ miles P/U from Burnbanks.

Haweswater Hotel, Lakeside Road, Bampton, CA10 2RP (713235): D/L: 2 miles P/U from Burnbanks.

Section 2 – Limestone Country

SHAP, PENRITH, CUMBRIA. TELEPHONE CODE: 01931

Brookfield, CA10 3PZ (716397): D/L.

Bulls Head Inn, Main Street, CA10 3NG (716678): C: D/L: Dogs.

Fell House, CA10 3NY (716343): D/L: Dogs: also General Store: P/U from Burnbanks/Rosgill.

Greyhound Hotel, Main Street (716474).

Kings Arms Hotel, Main Street, CA10 3NU (716277): Dogs.

New Ing Farm, CA10 3LX (716661): D/L.
1, The Rockery, CA10 3LY (716340).
Shap Well Hotel, CA10 3QU (716628): C: D/L: Dogs: 4 miles – Shap; 4 miles – Orton P/U.
Station Bunkhouse and Campsite (see under entry for Campsites and Bunkhouse Barns).

ORTON, PENRITH, CUMBRIA. TEL. CODE: 015396

Orton

The George Hotel, Front Street, Orton, CA10 3RJ (24229): D/L: Dogs.
The Old Barn, Bow Brow, Orton, CA10 3JS (24374)

Raisebeck

New House Farm, Raisebeck, Orton, CA10 3SD (24324): C: (plus caravan): Dogs, in caravan.

KIRKBY STEPHEN, CUMBRIA.

Newbiggin-on-Lune. Telephone Code: 015396

Tranna Hill, Newbiggin-on-Lune, CA17 4NY (23227): Non-smoking: ¾ mile – No P/U.

Kirkby Stephen. Telephone Code: 017683

Fletcher House, Fletcher Hill, CA17 4QQ (71013): D/L: Non-smoking.
Jolly Farmers House, 63 High Street, CA17 4SH (71063)L: D/L.
Kings Arms Hotel, Market Street, CA17 4QN (71378): D/L: Dogs.
Lockholme, 48 South Road, CA17 4SN (71321).
The Old Coach House, Faraday Road, CA17 4QL (71582)
Pennine View Caravan and Camping Park (see entry under Campsites).
Redmayne House, CA17 4RB (71441): D/L: Dogs: Non-smoking.

Section 3 – Into the Dales

RICHMOND, NORTH YORKSHIRE. TELEPHONE CODE: 01748

Keld

Frith Lodge, West Stonesdale, DL11 6EB (886489): (GR 891031): D/L: Dogs: 1 mile (just up Tan Hill road) – P/U (Also operates taxi service).

Greenlands, DL11 6DY (886576).

Thwaite

Kearton Guest House, DL11 6DR (886277): D/L: I mile – No P/U.
Usha Gap Campsite (see under entry for Campsites).

Gunnerside

Oxnop Hall (Mrs Annie Porter), SL11 6JJ (886253): D/L: Non-smoking in
bedrooms: 2 miles from high level route; P/U not feasible

Low Row*

*On B6270, not far from Isles Bridge (Low level route)
Punch Bowl Inn, DL11 6PF (886233): B.

Reeth

The Black Bull Inn, DL11 6SZ (884213): Dogs.
The Buck Hotel, DL10 6SW (884210): D/L.
The Burgoyne Hotel, On the Green, DL11 6SN (884292): D/L: Non-smoking.
2 Bridge Terrace, DL11 6TP (884572): Non-smoking.
Elder Peak, Arkengarthdale Road, DL11 6QX (884770).
Hackney House, DL11 6TW (884302).
The Kings Arms, High Row, DL11 6SY (884259): D/L: Dogs.
The Olde Temperance, DL11 6TE (884626): D/L.
Walpardoe, Anvil Square, DL11 6TE (884626): D/L.

Marrick

The Lodge (David Trusson), DL11 7UQ (884474): Dogs: Non-smoking.

Section 4 – The Vale of Mowbray

RICHMOND, NORTH YORKSHIRE. TELEPHONE CODE: 01748

Richmond

Black Lion Hotel, Finkle Street, DL10 4QB (823121): D/L: Dogs.
The Buck Inn, Newbiggin, DL10 4DX (822259/850141).
Emanuel Guest House, 41 Maison Dieu, DL10 7DU (823584): D/L: Dogs.
Field View, 15 Queen's Road, DL10 4AI: D/L: Dogs.
The Frenchgate Hotel, 59/61 Frenchgate, DL10 7AE (822087/823596): D/L: Dogs
Mrs Sheila Lee, 27 Hurgill Road (824092). D/L.
The Old Brewery Guest House, 29 The Green, DL10 4RG (822460): D/L.
Pottergate Guest House, 4 Pottergate, DL10 4AB (823826): D/L: Non-smoking.

West Cottage, Victoria Road, DL10 4AS (824046): Non-smoking.
Willance House Guest House, 24 Frenchgate, DL10 7AG (824467): D/L: Dogs:
Non-smoking in bedrooms.
Windsor House, 9 Castle Hill, DL10 7AG (823285).
Mrs Sharon Woodward, 66 Frenchgate, DL10 7AG (823421): D/L: Dogs.

Brompton-on-Swale

Brompton Caravan and Camping Site (see under entry for Campsites).
The Tudor Hotel, Gatherly Road, DL10 7JF (818021): D/L: Dogs.

Catterick Bridge

Bridge House Hotel, DL10 7PE(818331): D/L: Dogs
The Farmers Arms, DL10 7HZ (818062): C: D/L.

Catterick Village

Rose Cottage Guest House, 26 High Street, DL10 7LJ (811164): D/L: Non-smoking: 1 mile P/U Catterick Bridge.

NORTHALLERTON, NORTH YORKSHIRE. TELEPHONE CODE: 01609

Danby Wiske

The White Swan Inn, DL7 0NQ (770122): C: Dogs.

Brompton

Hallikeld House, Stokesley Road, Brompton, DL6 2UE (773613): (GR 393969):
D/L: 1½ miles P/U.

East Rounton

Hollins Stables, East Rounton, DL6 2 LG (882695): C: D/L: 1½ miles P/U. Willing
to pick up and ferry walkers staying more than one night from points east and
west.

Northallerton

Alverton Guest House, 26 South Parade, DL7 8SG (776207): D/L: 3 miles P/U.

Ingleby Arncliffe

Monks House, DL6 3ND (882294): D/L: Non-smoking.

Ingleby Cross

Blue Bell Inn, DL6 3NF (882272): C: D/L.
North York Moors Adventure Centre, Park House, DL6 3PE (882571): C: D/L: Dogs.
Ox-Hill Farm, DL6 3NJ (882255): (GR 459015): Non-smoking: ½ mile – No P/U.

Section 5 – The North York Moors

NORTHALLERTON, NORTH YORKSHIRE.
TELEPHONE CODE: 01609

Osmotherly

Oak Garth Farm, North End, DL6 3BH (883314): D/L: Small dogs: Non-smoking:
1 mile No P/U.
The Queen Catherine Hotel, 7 West End, DL6 3AG (883209): D/L: Dogs: 1 mile P/U.

STOKESLEY, MIDDLESBROUGH, CLEVELAND.
TELEPHONE CODE: 01642

Chop Gate, Stokesley

1 Foresters Cottage, Chop Gate, Stokesley, TS9 7JD (778368).

Chop Gate, Bilsdale

Maltkiln House, Urra, Bilsdale, TS9 7LZ (778216).

Great Broughton

The Wainstones Hotel, Great Broughton, TS9 7EW (712268): D/L: Non-smoking:
1½ miles P/U.

Kirkby-in-Cleveland

Toft Hill Farm (see under entry for Campsites).
Dromonby Grange Farm, Kirkby-in-Cleveland, TS9 7AR (712227): D/L: Dogs:
1 mile P/U.
Dromonby Hall Farm, Busby Lane, Kirkby-in-Cleveland, TS9 7 AP (712312): D/L:
Non-smoking: 1 mile P/U.

DANBY, NORTH YORKSHIRE.
TELEPHONE CODE: 01287

Sycamore House, YO21 2NW (660125): C (GR 688056): D/L: Dogs: 2 ½ miles P/U from Lion Inn.

BLAKEY/BLAKEY RIDGE, KIRKBYMOORSIDE,
NORTH YORKSHIRE. TELEPHONE CODE: 01751

High Blakey House, Blakey, YO6 6LQ (417186): D/L: Non-smoking.
The Lion Inn, Blakey Ridge, YO6 6LQ (417320): C: D/L: Dogs.

WHITBY, NORTH YORKSHIRE.
TELEPHONE CODE: 01947

Glaisdale

Anglers Rest Inn, YO21 2QH (897261): C: D/L: Dogs.
The Arncliffe Arms, YO21 2QL (897209): D/L: Dogs.
Egton Banks Farm, YO21 2QP (897289): C: D/L: Dogs, by arrangement: ¾ mile P/U.
Hollins Farm, YO21 2PZ (897516: C (GR 753042): D/L: Dogs.
Red House Farm, YO21 2PZ (897242): D/L: Dogs, outside: Non-smoking.
Sycamore Dell, YO21 2PZ (897345): C: D/L: Non-smoking.

Egton Bridge

The Postgate Inn, YO21 1UX (895241): D/L: Dogs.

Grosmont

Eskdale, YO22 5PT (895385): D/L: Dogs.
Grosmont House, YO22 5PE (895539): C: D4 D/L: Non-smoking.
Hazelwood House, Front Street, YO22 5QE (895292): D/L: Dogs: Non-smoking.

High Hawkser

York House Private Hotel, YO22 4LW (880314): D/L.

Robin Hood's Bay

Devon House, Station Road, Robin Hood's Bay, YO22 4RL (880197): D/L: Non-smoking.
Hook's House Farm (see under entries for Campsites).

Meadowfield, Mount Pleasant North, Robin Hood's Bay (YO22 4RE (880564): D/L.

Middlewood Farm Holiday Park (see under entry from Campsites).

Muir Lea Stores, New Road, Robin Hood's Bay, YO22 4SG (880316): D/L: Non-smoking in bedrooms.

Rose Garth, Thorpe Lane, Robin Hood's Bay, YO22 4RN (880578): D/L.

Victoria Hotel, Station Road, Robin Hood's Bay, YO22 4Rl (880205): D/L.

Wayfarer Restaurant, Robin Hood's Bay, YO22 $RL (880240): D/L: Dogs: Non-smoking.

Spital Bridge

Harbour Grange (see under entry for Bunkhouse Barns).

Whitby

Ashford, 8 Royal Crescent, YO21 3EJ (602138): D/L: Dogs: 3 miles P/U.

CAMPSITES

The campsites listed below range from those with full facilities to nothing more than the opportunity to pitch a tent in the grounds of a bed and breakfast halt. Walkers intending to camp should check first what facilities are available.

In addition many farmers and landowners along the walk will permit one or two tents for a single overnight stay, but please make a point of obtaining permission before camping. If no separate details are given below of properties, please refer to the bed and breakfast guide.

Aikbank Cottage, SANDWITH, Whitehaven
Tarn Flatt Hall, SANDWITH, Whitehaven
Cohinorah Guest House, ST BEES
The Seacote Hotel, ST BEES
Stonehouse Farm, ST BEES
Fell View, 3 Cleator Gate, CLEATOR
The Old Vicarage, ENNERDALE
Ennerdale Village Campsite, High Bridge Farm, ENNERDALE, Cleator, Cumbria CA23 3AR (01946 861339)
Low Moor End Farm, ENNERDALE
Gillercombe (Chapel Farm Campsite), ROSTHWAITE, Borrowdale
Stonethwaite Farm, STONETHWAITE, Borrowdale
Broadrayne Farm, GRASMERE
Home Farm, PATTERDALE
Haweswater Hotel, Lakeside Road, BRAMPTON

Bulls Head Inn, SHAP

Green Farm, SHAP

Shap Wells Hotel, SHAP

The George Hotel, ORTON

New House Farm, RAISEBECK, Orton

Bents Farm, NEWBIGGIN-ON-LUNE, Kirkby Stephen

Pennine View Caravan and Camping Park, Station Road, KIRKBY STEPHEN, Cumbria CA17 4SZ (017683 71717)

Usha Gap Campsite, MUKER, Richmond, North Yorkshire DL11 6DW (01748 86214)

Manor House Farm, HEALAUGH, Richmond

Helmsley House, MARRICK, Richmond

Hillcrest, SLEEGILL, Richmond

Brompton Caravan and Camping Park, BROMPTON-ON-SWALE, Richmond, North Yorkshire DL10 7EZ (01749 824629)

Park House Farm, Parkgate Lane, BROMPTON-ON-SWALE, Richmond, North Yorkshire DL10 7HD (01748 818621)

The Farmers Arms, CATTERICK BRIDGE

Laylands Farm, BOLTON-ON-SWALE

The White Swan, DANBY WISKE

Hollins Stables, EAST ROUNTON

Lovesome Hill Farm, LOVESOME HILL

Blue Bell Inn, INGLEBY CROSS

North York Moors Adventure Centre, INGLEBY CROSS

Hemmelstones, Clack Lane, OSMOTHERLY

Beakhills Farm, CHOP GATE, Stokesley

Home Farm, Chop Gate, BILSDALE, Middlesbrough, Cleveland TS9 7HZ (01642 778343)

Toft Hill Farm (Mrs Joan Hughes), Kirkby, GREAT BROUGHTON, Cleveland TS9 7HJ (01642 712469)

Dromonby Hall Farm, KIRKBY-IN-CLEVELAND, Stokesley

Sycamore House, DANBY, Whitby

The Lion Inn, BLAKEY RIDGE

Anglers Rest Inn, GLAISDALE

Egton Banks Farm, GLAISDALE

Hollins Farm, GLAISDALE

Sycamore Dell, GLAISDALE

Grosmont House, GROSMONT

Woodside, Front Street, GROSMONT

Farsyde House, FYLINGTHORPE, Whitby

Hook's House Farm, ROBIN HOOD'S BAY, Whitby, North Yorkshire YO22 4PE (01947 880283)

Middlewood Farm Holiday Park. ROBIN HOOD'S BAY, Whitby, North Yorkshire YO22 4UF (01947 880414)

BUNKHOUSE BARNS

The provision of bunkhouse barns is a fairly recent initiative, aimed at providing simple, inexpensive accommodation with few facilities. The term Bunkhouse barn also includes camping barns, which are quite often rather more Spartan.

In all cases walkers should book such accommodation in advance, and check precisely what facilities are available. If no separate details are given below of proprietors, please refer to the bed and breakfast guide.

Tarn Flatt Hall, SANDWITH
Station Bunk House and Tent Site, SHAP (see under entry for Campsites)
Bents Farm, NEWBIGGIN-ON-LUNE, Kirkby Stephen
Ladthwaite Farm, Ladthwaite Farm (GR 797068), KIRKBY STEPHEN, Cumbria (017683 71488)
Punch Bowl Inn, LOW ROW, Richmond
Laylands Farm, BOLTON-ON-SWALE
Lovesome Hill Farm, LOVESOME HILL
Harbour Grange, Spital Bridge, WHITBY, North Yorkshire YO22 4EG (01947 600817)

YOUTH HOSTELS

The following youth hostels are on or near the Coast to Coast Walk. Full details of their opening times should be checked with the YHA Accommodation Guide.

BORROWDALE (GR254142), Longthwaite, Keswick, Cumbria CA12 5XE (0870 770 5870; Email: borrowdale@yha.org.uk)
ENNERDALE (HIGH GILLERTHWAITE)(GR142141), Cat Crag, Ennerdale, Cleator, Cumbria CA23 3AX (0870 770 5820; Email: ennerdale@yha.org.uk)
BLACK SAIL (GR194124), Black Sail Hut, Ennerdale, Cleator, Cumbria CA23 3AY (07711 108450)
HONISTER HAUSE (GR226135), Seatoller, Keswick, Cumbria CA12 5XN (0870 770 5870; Email: honister@yha.org.uk)
GRASMERE (BUTTERLIP HOW) (GR336077), Easedale Road, Grasmere, Ambleside, Cumbria LA22 9QG (0870 770 5836; Email: grasmere@yha.org.uk)

GRASMERE (THORNEY HOW) (GR 332084), Easedale Road, Grasmere, Ambleside, Cumbria LA22 9QG (0870 770 5836)

HELVELLYN (GR366173), Greenside, Glenridding, Penrith, Cumbria CA11 0QR (0870 770 5862; Email: helvellyn@yha.org.uk)

PATTERDALE (GR399156), Goldrill House, Patterdale, Penrith, Cumbria CA11 0NW (0870 770 5986; Email: patterdale@yha.org.uk)

KIRKBY STEPHEN (GR774085), Market Street, Kirkby Stephen, Cumbria CA17 4QQ (0870 770 5904; Email: kirkbystephen@yha.org.uk)

KELD (GR891009), Upper Swaledale, Richmond, North Yorkshire DL11 6LL (0870 770 5888)

GRINTON (GR048975), Grinton, Richmond, North Yorkshire DL11 6HS (0870 770 5844; Email: grinton@yha.org.uk)

OSMOTHERLY (GR461981), Core Ghyll, Osmotherly, Northallerton, North Yorkshire DL6 3AH (0870 770 5982; Email: osmotherly@yha.org.uk)

BOGGLE HOLE (GR954040), Boggle Hole, Mill Beck, Fylingthorpe, Whitby, North Yorkshire YO22 4UQ (0870 770 5704; Email: bogglehole@yha.org.uk)

WHITBY (GR 902111), East Cliff, Whitby, North Yorkshire YO22 4JT (0870 770 6088; Email: whitby@yha.org.uk)

APPENDIX 2: DOCTORS AND DENTISTS

There is no desire to wish on walkers the ills that doctors and dentists might need to cure, but these things happen. The following doctors and dentists indicated their willingness to treat Coast to Coast walkers. Surgery hours vary considerably, and so it is always better to telephone ahead to be sure of treatment.

Doctors

Dr S Bagshaw and Partners, 27–28 Church Street, WHITEHAVEN, Cumbria CA28 7EB (01946 693660)

Dr Sydney and Partners, Flatt Walks Health Centre, WHITEHAVEN, Cumbria CA28 7RJ (01946 692173). Branch surgery at CLEATOR MOOR (01946 810304)

Dr Proudfoot and Partners, 3 Catherine Street, WHITEHAVEN, Cumbria CA28 7PD (01946 693094)

Dr G J Ironside, 22 Irish Street, WHITEHAVEN, Cumbria CA27 7BU (01946 694457)

Dr A P Timney and Partner, 17 Irish Street, WHITEHAVEN, Cumbria CA28 7BU (01946 693412)

Drs Gallacher and Creed, Westcroft House, 66 Main Street, EGREMONT, Cumbria CA22 2DB (01946 820348). Branch surgery at CLEATOR MOOR (01946 813240)

Dr J W Veitch and Partners, Beech House, Main Street, EGREMONT, Cumbria CA22 2DB (01946 820203/820214). Branch surgeries, limited service, at ST BEES (Tuesday and Friday, 10.00 am – 11.00 am) (01946 822689), and CLEATOR MOOR (Monday and Friday, 9.00 am – 11.00 am and 4.00 pm – 5.30 pm, plus Saturday, 9.30 am – 10.00 am)

Dr Clifford and Dr Judith Atack, The Surgery, 9 Bank Street, KESWICK, Cumbria CA12 5JY (017687 72438)

Dr Hamilton and Partners, Castlehead Medical Centre, Ambleside Road, KESWICK, Cumbria CA12 4DB (017687 72025)

Dr P Walker and Partner, The Surgery, West Lane, SHAP, Cumbria CA10 3LT (01931 716230)

Dr C S M Hallam and Dr S Huck, The Health Centre, Silver Street, KIRKBY STEPHEN, Cumbria CA17 4RB (017683 71369)

Dr Ginns and Partners, The Quakers Lane Surgery, RICHMOND, North Yorkshire DL10 4BB (01748 850440)

Dr Hodgson and Dr Kearney, Bridge House Surgery, Aldbrough St John, RICHMOND, North Yorkshire DL11 7SZ (01325 374332)

Drs Gibson, Patterson and Pearson, 1/3 Queens Road, RICHMOND, North Yorkshire DL10 4AH (01748 822306)

Dr Crookshank and Partners, Mowbray House Surgery, 277 North End, NORTHALLERTON, North Yorkshire DL7 8DP (01609 775281)

Dentists

Mr R Broad and Partner, 74 High Street, CLEATOR MOOR, Cumbria, CA25 5 BL (01946 812383)

Mr David G Watt, Market Square, KIRKBY STEPHEN, Cumbria, CA17 4QT (017683 71250)

Dr A D Pope and Associates, 5 Rosemary Lane, RICHMOND, North Yorkshire, DL10 4DP (01748 824177)

Malpas House Dental Surgeons, Malpas House, 11 South Parade, NORTHALLERTON, North Yorkshire, DL7 8SE (01609 772549)

APPENDIX 3: USEFUL ADDRESSES

Youth Hostel Association

Trevelyan House, Dimple Road, Matlock, Derbyshire DE4 3YH. Tel: 0870 870 8808; Email: customerservice@yha.org.uk; Website: www.yha.org.uk.

Tourist Boards

Cumbria Tourist Board, Ashleigh, Holly Road, Windermere, Cumbria LA23 2AQ. Tel: 015394 44444; Fax: 015394 44041; Email: mail@cumbria-tourist-board.co.uk; Website: www.gocumbria.co.uk.
Yorkshire Tourist Board, 312 Tadcaster Road, York, North Yorkshire YO24 1GS. Tel: 01904 701100; Fax: 01904 701414; Email: mail@ytb.org.uk; Website: www.ytb.org.uk.

National Park Authorities

Lake District National Park Visitor Services, Brockhole, Windermere, Cumbria, LA23 1LJ (015394 46601).
Yorkshire Dales National Park, Colvend, Hebden Road, Grassington, Skipton, North Yorkshire, BD23 5LB (01756 752748).
North York Moors National Park, The Old Vicarage, Bondgate, Helmsley, York, YO6 5BP (01439 70657).

Tourist Information Offices

(NOTE: Not all the following offices are open throughout the year. Do check first, if you intend to use them.)

Egremont: 12 Main Street, Egremont, Cumbria CA22 2DW (01946 820693)
Seatoller: Seatoller Barn, Seatoller, Borrowdale, Keswick, Cumbria CA12 5XN (017687 77294)
Grasmere: Redbank Road, Grasmere, Cumbria LA22 9SW (015394 35245)
Kirkby Stephen: Market Square, Kirkby Stephen, Cumbria CA17 4QN (017683 71199)
Richmond: Friary Gardens, Victoria Road, Richmond, North Yorkshire DL10 4AJ (01748 850252)
Northallerton: The Applegarth Car Park, Northallerton, North Yorkshire DL7 8LZ (01609 776864)
The Moors Centre, Danby Lodge, Lodge Lane, Whitby, North Yorkshire YO21 2NB (01287 660654)
Whitby: Langhorne Road, Whitby, North Yorkshire YO21 1YN (01947 602674)

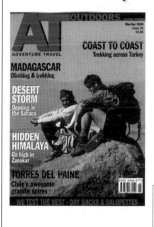

LISTING OF CICERONE GUIDES

NORTHERN ENGLAND
LONG DISTANCE TRAILS
- THE DALES WAY
- THE ISLE OF MAN COASTAL PATH
- THE PENNINE WAY
- THE ALTERNATIVE COAST TO COAST
- NORTHERN COAST-TO-COAST WALK
- THE RELATIVE HILLS OF BRITAIN
- MOUNTAINS ENGLAND & WALES
  VOL 1 WALES
  VOL 2 ENGLAND

CYCLING
- BORDER COUNTRY BIKE ROUTES
- THE CHESHIRE CYCLE WAY
- THE CUMBRIA CYCLE WAY
- THE DANUBE CYCLE WAY
- LANDS END TO JOHN O'GROATS
  CYCLE GUIDE
- ON THE RUFFSTUFF
  84 BIKE RIDES IN NORTH ENGLAND
- RURAL RIDES NO.1 WEST SURREY
- RURAL RIDES NO.1 EAST SURREY
- SOUTH LAKELAND CYCLE RIDES
- THE WAY OF ST JAMES
  LE PUY TO SANTIAGO – CYCLIST'S

LAKE DISTRICT AND
MORECAMBE BAY
- CONISTON COPPER MINES
- CUMBRIA WAY & ALLERDALE
  RAMBLE
- THE CHRONICLES OF MILNTHORPE
- THE EDEN WAY
- FROM FELL AND FIELD
- KENDAL – A SOCIAL HISTORY
- A LAKE DISTRICT ANGLER'S GUIDE
- LAKELAND TOWNS
- LAKELAND VILLAGES
- LAKELAND PANORAMAS
- THE LOST RESORT?
- SCRAMBLES IN THE LAKE DISTRICT
- MORE SCRAMBLES IN THE
  LAKE DISTRICT
- SHORT WALKS IN LAKELAND
  BOOK 1: SOUTH
  BOOK 2: NORTH
  BOOK 3: WEST
- ROCKY RAMBLER'S WILD WALKS
- RAIN OR SHINE
- ROADS AND TRACKS OF THE
  LAKE DISTRICT
- THE TARNS OF LAKELAND
  VOL 1: WEST
- THE TARNS OF LAKELAND VOL 2:
  EAST
- WALKING ROUND THE LAKES
- WALKS SILVERDALE/ARNSIDE
- WINTER CLIMBS IN LAKE DISTRICT

NORTH-WEST ENGLAND
- WALKING IN CHESHIRE
- FAMILY WALKS IN FOREST OF
  BOWLAND

- WALKING IN THE FOREST OF
  BOWLAND
- LANCASTER CANAL WALKS
- WALKER'S GUIDE TO LANCASTER
  CANAL
- CANAL WALKS VOL 1: NORTH
- WALKS FROM THE LEEDS-
  LIVERPOOL CANAL
- THE RIBBLE WAY
- WALKS IN RIBBLE COUNTRY
- WALKING IN LANCASHIRE
- WALKS ON THE WEST PENNINE
  MOORS
- WALKS IN LANCASHIRE WITCH
  COUNTRY
- HADRIAN'S WALL
  VOL 1 : THE WALL WALK
  VOL 2 : WALL COUNTRY WALKS

NORTH-EAST ENGLAND
- NORTH YORKS MOORS
- THE REIVER'S WAY
- THE TEESDALE WAY
- WALKING IN COUNTY DURHAM
- WALKING IN THE NORTH PENNINES
- WALKING IN NORTHUMBERLAND
- WALKING IN THE WOLDS
- WALKS IN THE NORTH YORK
  MOORS BOOKS 1 AND 2
- WALKS IN THE YORKSHIRE DALES
  BOOKS 1,2 AND 3
- WALKS IN DALES COUNTRY
- WATERFALL WALKS – TEESDALE &
  HIGH PENNINES
- THE YORKSHIRE DALES
- YORKSHIRE DALES ANGLER'S GUIDE

THE PEAK DISTRICT
- STAR FAMILY WALKS PEAK
  DISTRICT/STH YORKS
- HIGH PEAK WALKS
- WEEKEND WALKS IN THE PEAK
  DISTRICT
- WHITE PEAK WALKS
  VOL.1 NORTHERN DALES
  VOL.2 SOUTHERN DALES
- WHITE PEAK WAY
- WALKING IN PEAKLAND
- WALKING IN SHERWOOD FOREST
- WALKING IN STAFFORDSHIRE
- THE VIKING WAY

WALES AND WELSH BORDERS
- ANGLESEY COAST WALKS
- ASCENT OF SNOWDON
- THE BRECON BEACONS
- CLWYD ROCK
- HEREFORD & THE WYE VALLEY
- HILLWALKING IN SNOWDONIA
- HILLWALKING IN WALES VOL.1
- HILLWALKING IN WALES VOL.2
- LLEYN PENINSULA COASTAL PATH
- WALKING OFFA'S DYKE PATH
- THE PEMBROKESHIRE COASTAL
  PATH

- THE RIDGES OF SNOWDONIA
- SARN HELEN
- SCRAMBLES IN SNOWDONIA
- SEVERN WALKS
- THE SHROPSHIRE HILLS
- THE SHROPSHIRE WAY
- SPIRIT PATHS OF WALES
- WALKING DOWN THE WYE
- A WELSH COAST TO COAST WALK
- WELSH WINTER CLIMBS

THE MIDLANDS
- CANAL WALKS VOL 2: MIDLANDS
- THE COTSWOLD WAY
- COTSWOLD WALKS
  BOOK 1: NORTH
  BOOK 2: CENTRAL
  BOOK 3: SOUTH
- THE GRAND UNION CANAL WALK
- HEART OF ENGLAND WALKS
- WALKING IN OXFORDSHIRE
- WALKING IN WARWICKSHIRE
- WALKING IN WORCESTERSHIRE
- WEST MIDLANDS ROCK

SOUTH AND SOUTH-WEST
ENGLAND
- WALKING IN BEDFORDSHIRE
- WALKING IN BUCKINGHAMSHIRE
- CHANNEL ISLAND WALKS
- CORNISH ROCK
- WALKING IN CORNWALL
- WALKING IN THE CHILTERNS
- WALKING ON DARTMOOR
- WALKING IN DEVON
- WALKING IN DORSET
- CANAL WALKS VOL 3: SOUTH
- EXMOOR & THE QUANTOCKS
- THE GREATER RIDGEWAY
- WALKING IN HAMPSHIRE
- THE ISLE OF WIGHT
- THE KENNET & AVON WALK
- THE LEA VALLEY WALK
- LONDON THEME WALKS
- THE NORTH DOWNS WAY
- THE SOUTH DOWNS WAY
- THE ISLES OF SCILLY
- THE SOUTHERN COAST TO COAST
- SOUTH WEST WAY
  VOL.1 MINEH'D TO PENZ.
  VOL.2 PENZ. TO POOLE
- WALKING IN SOMERSET
- WALKING IN SUSSEX
- THE THAMES PATH
- TWO MOORS WAY
- WALKS IN KENT BOOK 1
- WALKS IN KENT BOOK 2
- THE WEALDWAY & VANGUARD WAY

SCOTLAND
- WALKING IN THE ISLE OF ARRAN
- THE BORDER COUNTRY –
  A WALKERS GUIDE
- BORDER COUNTRY CYCLE ROUTES

Cicerone's mission is to inform and inspire by providing the best guides to exploring the world

Since its foundation over 30 years ago, Cicerone has specialised in publishing guidebooks and has built a reputation for quality and reliability. It now publishes nearly 300 guides to the major destinations for outdoor enthusiasts, including Europe, UK and the rest of the world.

Written by leading and committed specialists, Cicerone guides are recognised as the most authoritative. They are full of information, maps and illustrations so that the user can plan and complete a successful and safe trip or expedition – be it a long face climb, a walk over Lakeland fells, an alpine traverse, a Himalayan trek or a ramble in the countryside.

With a thorough introduction to assist planning, clear diagrams, maps and colour photographs to illustrate the terrain and route, and accurate and detailed text, Cicerone guides are designed for ease of use and access to the information.

If the facts on the ground change, or there is any aspect of a guide that you think we can improve, we are always delighted to hear from you.

Cicerone Press
2 Police Square Milnthorpe Cumbria LA7 7PY
Tel:01539 562 069   Fax:01539 563 417
e-mail:info@cicerone.co.uk   web:www.cicerone.co.uk

CICERONE